ITEMS MAY HAVE SHIFTED

WHEN MISSIONARIES GET REROUTED

MAXINE McDONALD

FOREWORD BY STEVE RICHARDSON

Items May Have Shifted: When Missionaries Get Rerouted
by Maxine McDonald

© 2023 Pioneers-USA
ISBN: 9781735234557

Cover Design: Karina Kolman
Cover Photo: LALASZA on Unsplash

Unless otherwise noted, Scripture quotations are taken from THE ENGLISH STANDARD VERSION. © 2001 by Crossway Bibles, a division of Good News Publishers.

Contents

A Note to Readers..5

Foreword 7

Introduction 9

All In, From Billboard to Precipice
Zach & Denise Gregg's Story 13

Lands of Milk & Honey
Frank & Eileen Goodman's Story............................35

Lands of Tea & Opportunity
Kristi Reid's Story 59

Available, Brave & Crazy
Dave & Ashley Moore's Story.................................89

Of War & Wallpaper
James & Lisa Walker's Story...................................111

Epilogue...139

Lisa Walker's Dill Pickle Soup Recipe 141

About the Author 145

A Note to Readers

THIS IS A BOOK of true stories about the experiences of Pioneers missionaries—stories we hear echoed by cross-cultural workers sent by many organizations to and from countries all over the world. The names of people and places and some identifying details have been intentionally altered to protect missionaries, local believers and the communities they serve. Modifying some of the specifics allows us to publicly share stories of God at work in unlikely places. We invite you to join us in celebrating His faithfulness and extending His invitation of blessing to all people.

Foreword

HAVE YOU EVER ASKED God to use you, thinking you knew what that would look like, and then had Him do something completely unexpected? Sometimes, when we step out in faith, things seem to go wrong. Plans fail. Opportunities evaporate. Ministries collapse. When that happens, it's easy to get disoriented or disillusioned. We are confronted again and again with threshold moments, intersections of life where we must decide, *How will I respond?*

Because global missions—making disciples of all the peoples of the world—is such a vast and complex task, we sometimes assume, Faithful missionaries are the ones who go somewhere and stay for the rest of their lives. Longevity has been a primary goal and remains appropriate and necessary in many contexts, but God is now moving His workforce around the globe with increasing frequency. It's becoming somewhat rare for a missionary to spend a lifetime in just one location.

Scripture is full of examples of displaced people and unexpected transitions. Think of Abraham, Jonah, Daniel and the Apostle Paul. Joseph was relocated by force. Moses spent 40 years in the desert of Midian learning his way around in preparation for what we now consider a far more fruitful season of ministry leading the people of Israel out of slavery. And think about how devastated the disciples must have been to see Jesus crucified! From their perspective, God's plan to provide a Messiah had clearly been shattered irreparably. But then God revealed that apparent defeat was an essential part of His greatest victory. Throughout history, mobility and surprise have been built into His redemptive plans. God's people have always been on the move.

This book presents a rich and multifaceted picture of faithfulness on the mission field. We hear how missionaries have navigated the tension between perseverance in what God called them to do and flexibility when their plans were disrupted. Reflecting on these stories, I realized how much I've experienced the same dynamics. My own journey in missions has had its share of surprises. I find it both inspiring and reassuring to recognize that God not only allows us to bear enduring fruit in each season of ministry, however long or short, but He simultaneously transforms our own hearts and prepares us for future stages of fruitfulness in other settings.

Stories of displaced and rerouted missionaries remind us that our sovereign God orchestrates all the threads of our lives. Nothing is wasted in His economy as we prayerfully seek Him even—and maybe especially—in situations beyond our control and understanding. I believe that a certain recognition, and perhaps honor, is due to missionaries who have paid a price to establish a life and ministry in one setting and then are willing to start over, whether in their home country or abroad when circumstances require it.

In some ways, this book is a compilation of stories of shattered dreams that, in retrospect, turned out to be God-glorifying examples of answered prayer. Whether you (or missionaries you care about) are on the move by necessity or by choice, remember that God's people are called to a flexible, responsive faithfulness, tenaciously clinging to the God of the unexpected.

— *Steve Richardson*
President, Pioneers-USA

Introduction

ON FEBRUARY 24TH, 2022, James and Lisa Walker woke to find Central Europe bracing for war. In their town, just an hour from the border with Ukraine, gas stations and ATMs were soon overrun, and fighter jets roared overhead at alarmingly frequent intervals. Tens of thousands of Ukrainian refugees—who would grow to millions in the coming weeks—streamed across the border in the Walkers' direction.

On February 25th, Lisa dug through their closets for spare linens while James made the first of what would be dozens of trips to the border. That night, 31 refugees stayed in their home, including a family of five with a small dog. The oldest daughter, a teenager, spoke English well and helped her parents share some of their story with James and Lisa. The father pastored a church in Ukraine, but the family was Latvian. They had served as missionaries to a Turkic minority people group in another country in the former Soviet Union since the 1990s. In 2021, the father had been declared a "Danger to the Republic" and deported. They fled to Ukraine and established a new ministry there. Now they were fleeing again.

James and Lisa listened to the story in shock, not just because of what the family had been through but also because they had been through some of the same things. By 2022, the Walkers had worked as missionaries in Central Europe for more than two decades and were deeply rooted in the local community. But James and Lisa didn't start off in Central Europe. They were rerouted there.

In the mid-90s, the Walkers had set out to be missionaries to the same Turkic minority group in the same former Soviet republic as their Latvian guests. After five years of ministry, James had also been declared a "Danger to the Republic" and deported. The Walkers started over in Central Europe. After hearing their overlapping story, the pastor's wife told Lisa with mock dismay, "I don't know if I'm going to be able to sleep in your house tonight with all these 'dangerous' men around!" Then she gripped both of Lisa's hands and told her, "We never fully understand why, but I think the Lord sent you to the former Soviet Union all those years ago, if nothing else, to receive our family today."

This book is a collection of stories of missionaries who, like the Walkers and their Latvian guests, left everything and moved across the world to serve the unreached and then were rerouted to a completely different location. Their experiences illustrate an inherent tension missionaries must maintain in today's chaotic world: the commitment to go deep in difficult contexts as if it's forever and the openhandedness to accept that God may disrupt their plans at any moment.

A lot of Christians think of missionaries as people who pack up and move abroad, but we may not realize how many of them do that more than once. Fully half of Pioneers-USA missionaries (those sent out from the US) who have served on the field for 10 years or more have changed countries at least once. And that doesn't include those who switched locations before they made it to the field in the first place or returned to serve at our sending base.

In orientation and training programs for long-term mission- aries, you don't hear a lot of talk about changing fields, and for good reason. It's hard to dive deeply into the language and culture of the people you plan to serve if you always have an eye on the exit. But the truth is, a lot of missionaries aren't able to stay as long as they hope in their fields of service. Some step away from cross-cultural ministry completely. Others start over somewhere else.

A lot of rerouted missionaries find new purposes and fruitful ministries serving displaced people, which there are more of today than ever before. The UN estimates that in 2022, 100 million people were driven from their homes by violence, conflict, corruption and persecution.[1] The largest groups fled from Ukraine, Myanmar, Syria, Burkina Faso, Ethiopia and Yemen. Displaced missionaries are often able to connect quickly and deeply with refugees because of their shared experience of loss and starting over in an unfamiliar place. A growing number of people are also moving internationally for reasons besides war or famine (like jobs or education). More than 280 million people currently live outside their country of birth, a three-fold increase since 1970.[2] James and Lisa Walker are part of a tiny subset of people who move cross-culturally to share the gospel.

During the first months of the war in Ukraine, the Walkers hosted more than 150 people and their pets. Amid all that chaos, the conversation with the Latvian family displaced from both a Soviet republic and Ukraine stands out to Lisa. She doesn't feel she deserves credit for helping them. "I didn't do anything special. The Lord did it. He allowed us to be at the border and for their family to pass through and have a place to rest." And God blessed Lisa through that

---

1. United Nations. UN News: Global Perspective Human Stories. December 26, 2022. *https://news.un.org/en/story/2022/12/1131957.* Accessed May 26, 2023.

2. International Organization on Migration: UN Migration. World Migration Report 2022. *https://worldmigrationreport.iom.int/wmr-2022-interactive/.* Accessed May 26, 2023.

refugee family, whispering to her, *This is my purpose. This is what I have for you right now.*

God is unchanging in His character and faithful to His promises. He also upends our expectations, plans, lives and entire nations much more often than most of us would prefer. He keeps His people on the move, always with a purpose, but often without much warning or explanation. As Lisa puts it, "I need to hold my plans, my methods, the way I go about ministry very loosely. I don't understand the big picture, but I have to trust the One who does." And James agrees, "We have to just say, *God, You know what we need. We put ourselves in Your hands.* It's hard, and I don't know what else to say."

The Walkers' perspective echoes an ancient, but still very relevant, prayer: "We do not know what to do, but our eyes are on you" (2 Chronicles 20:12). May we continue to show the same humility and faith as we carry good news to a turbulent world.

All in, From Billboard to Precipice

Zach & Denise Gregg's Story
Part 1

HIS STORY

While eating at Taco Bell late one night during college, Zach Gregg noticed a "Volunteer Firefighters Needed" billboard outside the window. The next day, he signed up for a firefighter accreditation course which launched his career at one of the busiest fire stations in Georgia. Around the same time, a man from his church began modeling what it meant to follow Jesus in daily life. Zach decided, *whatever else I do, I have to do life-on-life discipleship with men like this.*

Zach's life revolved around firefighting and discipleship until another "billboard moment" rocked his world. During an otherwise ordinary Sunday morning sermon, his pastor explained that three billion people didn't yet have access to the gospel. The lack of witness among the unreached was, to Zach, one of those things "you just can't unhear." He had always thought of missionaries as "just a bunch of weird people, typically with long hair and lots of children."

But after that sermon, he dove into Scripture and was shocked to see the theme of global missions running through familiar texts from Genesis to Revelation. Suddenly his mindset changed from *Should I go?* to *Why would I not go?*

The next Sunday, Zach told his pastor, "I have to do something about the unreached, but I have no idea where to start." The pastor suggested he contact a missionary couple who, by God's providence, happened to be in town. Over lunch the next day, Mark and Alice Adams spent three hours unpacking the basics of global missions. Zach couldn't have gotten a crash course from a better source. Mark and Alice had extensive field experience in East Asia and were part of the international leadership of a missionary-sending organization called Pioneers. They encouraged Zach to go on some short-term mission trips to see what the Lord might have for him in the long term.

A few months later, Zach ventured into the Amazon, traveling on puddle-jumper planes between grass airstrips. On his first night in a remote village, Zach's missionary host knocked on his door. "You're an EMT, right?" she said, "Can you help deliver a baby?" That night, Zach started to really believe that the Lord could use a firefighter from Georgia to make disciples on the mission field. "It blew my mind that the two could ever come together."

Zach came away from his next trip, this time to Central Africa, with mixed emotions. He was both intimidated by the realities of life on the field and exuberant that the Lord would consider him to be a part of the work. Back at the fire station headquarters, he heard a co-worker say, "I've been here 10 years. Only 20-something more to go." Zach realized then that a career as a firefighter wasn't what God wanted for him. He called Mark and said, "I'm in for the long haul."

Zach's church invited him to give an informal presentation about his experience in Central Africa during a Sunday morning service. As he chatted with people afterward, a friend walked up with a beautiful young woman and said, "Denise, this is Zach. Zach, this is Denise, and she wants to go overseas." Then Zach's friend took a deliberate step backward and waited expectantly. And so, with no warning and a lot of awkwardness, Zach and Denise were officially introduced.

HER STORY

Like Zach, Denise grew up in a small town in Georgia with a church on every corner. As a child, she heard tales of missionaries like Lottie Moon and Annie Armstrong. As a freshman in high school, she took a short-term trip to Guatemala and came home determined to become a missionary herself. Denise's parents were less convinced. They supported missions as a good thing for other people to do but expected *their* little girl to work a good job, have a nice car and sit with them in church every Sunday.

But it was too late. Denise's eyes were open to the needs of the world and she went back to Guatemala every spring break. Her early understanding of missions was limited to meeting physical needs and telling Bible stories along the way. After a few years, she discovered the concept of unreached people groups and thought, *How could there be people who haven't ever heard the gospel?*

During college, a friend discipled Denise with the same life-on-life principles Zach had experienced and embraced. Denise got to see the way this woman honored her husband in daily life, saw her cry over cookies that didn't turn out right, and watched her get angry, then ask for forgiveness. All the good stuff, all the bad stuff, and in the middle of it all they talked about the Word and how it applied to their lives. Denise thought, *This is so cool! This is the Church.*

One day, Denise's mentor commented that a group of guys from their church would be returning soon from a trip to Central Africa.

The fateful morning of Zach's presentation, Denise didn't realize what was happening until she had been somewhat formally presented to him and left standing awkwardly in the center of a circle of expectant people. *There's no getting out of this*, she realized. Fortunately, Zach was quick on his feet and offered to connect her with some of the missionaries he had met on his trip.

THEIR STORY

Zach swears he played it cool after the church encounter, but he was clearly smitten. After a few months of inviting Denise to flag football games, tailgate parties and group dinners, he asked her to join him at a missions conference at Pioneers, the mission agency Mark and Alice had introduced him to. On the first night they were there, Denise shared her testimony, and it was yet another billboard moment for Zach. Afterward, he told a friend, "I'm pursuing Denise for marriage. I don't know if she'll have me, but I've got to try."

Zach and Denise officially started dating in March 2011. They traveled abroad separately over the summer, trying to discern where the Lord might have them serve, either individually or together. Denise already spoke Spanish, so South America seemed like a natural fit. However, her summer outreach program assigned her to a team traveling through Asia. She was surprised to find that she loved Asia even though it felt so much darker than anything she'd experienced on the Western side of the world. Denise thought, *Oh no! I want to go to Asia now, and Zach's probably still thinking about South America.* Little did she know, Zach was also drawn to Asia and worried about Denise's response. One of their first conversations when they finally met face-to-face again started with an awkward, "So...Asia...," and then relief as they realized, "Wait, you too?"

Zach and Denise became Mr. and Mrs. Gregg in March of 2012,

just a few months after they both joined Pioneers. They bought a globe and a copy of *Operation World: The Definitive Prayer Guide to Every Nation* and started praying about where in Asia God might want to use them. They also attended conferences, talked to missions organizations and sought advice from mentors. Soon, a presentation about the many Muslim peoples of East Asia drew Zach and Denise's attention. As they learned more, they felt increasingly certain that God wanted them to serve a particular Muslim minority group. As Denise puts it, "We didn't know, but we were pretty sure."

At that point, Mark Adams, Zach's original missions coach, invited them on a survey trip—a tour across East Asia, including the area where they planned to serve. On that trip, the Greggs met missionaries of all stripes: businesspeople, teachers, coffee producers, doctors, moms and artists. The diversity of these gospel workers inspired Zach and Denise. Surely God had a place for them as well.

At the very end of the trip, in a final conversation a half-hour before Zach and Denise left for the airport to fly home, they heard about 33 people groups clustered around a city called Daiji in the one area of the country they had not visited. Not only were those people groups unreached, no one had yet begun attempting to reach them. At the airport waiting for their first flight back to Georgia, Zach and Denise had another awkward start to a conversation. "So… those 33 people groups…"

One of the traits of God that the Greggs love is that He often stands His followers on a precipice. We know He will work and be faithful and put us right where He wants us, but we never know how He will do it. Zach and Denise were both ready to step off the precipice and move to Daiji.

Zach told the Lord, *I am all in for as long as You have me there.*

This is it, Denise agreed. *God told us. I'm committed until I die.*

READY, SET, GO

Before Zach and Denise could leave for the field as missionaries, they had to build a team of prayer and financial supporters to sustain them in ministry for the long term. They spent about a year in the U.S. sharing their ministry vision with family, friends and churches. They planned to focus on one or more of the 33 people groups that did not yet have a gospel witness in the area around the city of Daiji. As they built relationships, they hoped to share the gospel, disciple new believers and help them form new churches.

To the Greggs, it was obvious this would be a long-term project. It would take years just to learn the language to a high-enough proficiency to engage people on a spiritual level. But not everyone understood that. People often asked them, "How long are you going for?" Zach and Denise would answer, "We don't know. Until the Lord re-directs our steps, but we're going for the long haul." Even so, many seemed to expect them to come back after a year or two overseas.

During the preparation and support-raising process, the Greggs realized God wasn't just shaping and growing their own hearts in preparation for ministry to the unreached. He was also working in their parents, who shed a lot of tears as they let go of their dreams of having Zach and Denise and future grandkids close by. Just before the Greggs left for the field, Denise's mom expressed the bittersweetness. "You want your kids to follow the Lord and go wherever He takes them, but I didn't think it was going to be around the world." For Zach, it was an important reminder. "When you embark on this cross-cultural journey, sometimes you don't think about the impact God is having on so many other hearts and souls."

Zach and Denise left for the field a few days before their first anniversary, ready for a lifetime of service, sacrifice and adventure.

TAKING THE LEAP

The Greggs set about establishing a life in Daiji, home to half a million people—a tiny, obscure town by East Asian standards. A common saying about Daiji went like this: "There are no three days of sunshine together, no three honest men together and no three pennies to rub together." The city had a reputation as a dreary, backwoods place with dishonest people trapped in perpetual poverty. Zach and Denise planned to study the national language at a university there for two years before moving into full-time ministry in a more rural area nearby.

Daiji lay in a narrow river valley compressed from both sides by lush green mountains. The entire city seemed constantly under construction. With no room to expand outward, it strained upward. Ornate historic buildings were systematically torn down to make room for concrete tower blocks. Daiji illustrated the chaos and extreme economic disparity of rapid modernization. It had skyscrapers, but no airport. Widescreen TVs glowed from the open windows of thatched huts. Donkey carts vied with Maseratis for parking spaces. To Zach and Denise, "It was awesome. We loved it."

At least, they loved it eventually. The "country comes to town" atmosphere of Daiji meant most people had never seen a foreigner. Zach and Denise's white skin and light hair shocked people. They were stared at constantly. Every conversation began with the same questions: "Where are you from? Why are you here? How much money do you make?" The entire city smelled like tofu. The first apartment they saw as an option to rent was dirty, dimly lit and overrun by rats. They eventually settled in a reasonably nice place but struggled to make it home.

Since Zach and Denise planned to move overseas even before getting married, they had never really set up a house and didn't know how to do that, especially in the podunk-village-turned-concrete-jungle setting of Daiji. Denise felt guilty spending money on anything but necessities, worried that people would judge her. She cried a lot in the first year. Zach was terrified he wouldn't be able to learn the language. Some days he wanted to chuck his notebook off the balcony in frustration. Zach and Denise both love going deep with people, but until they learned the language and culture, they couldn't. The isolation of Daiji wore on them. For years they never even heard airplanes pass overhead. "God brought us to a very obscure place," Denise remembers, "He was tearing us down to build us up in Him. There was a lot of good, just for our souls, in moving to Daiji."

Fortunately, Zach and Denise had each other. When one of them felt discouraged, the other could offer perspective. They shared their hurt and frustration without feeling ashamed. About a year after arriving, the Greggs went to a conference. An experienced leader made a passing comment: "You're never married to East Asia. You're just married to Jesus." For reasons Denise can't explain, that statement gave her an immediate sense of relief. She finally felt free to make Daiji home, realizing *It's okay to put down roots even though it's painful to pull them up sometimes.*

STICKING THE LANDING

Zach and Denise finally began to settle. They realized that cooking was an essential part of hospitality for Denise, so they invested in kitchen items. Over time, they decorated their house with comfortable furniture and an abundance of pillows. They developed a date night routine, made pancakes every Saturday morning and watched *Remember the Titans* to celebrate the start of football season.

Gradually, the Greggs developed the deep relationships with local people that they had longed for. One afternoon, Zach sat at the kitchen table with one of his best friends, a local believer, reading 1 Peter 3 and discussing what it meant to live with their wives "in an understanding way" (1 Peter 3:7). The thought struck him, *Man, I love this so much! You could pull away our nationalities, and we are just two brothers loving the Word and wanting to apply it to our lives.* Denise remembers sitting at that same round, wooden table studying English from the *Jesus Storybook Bible* with students. They had so many questions about what they read. A friend who taught at a local preschool had always displayed a gentleness that Zach and Denise loved. She came for dinner one night and began asking them about what happens after we die. It's a topic that isn't usually discussed in East Asian culture, so the Greggs were surprised at her interest. A week later she came to know the Lord through another believer.

Denise often wrote Bible verses on the tile walls of her kitchen using a dry-erase marker. One day an unbelieving friend told her, "I want to know what that sentence on your wall means: *Man does not live by bread alone, but man lives by every word that comes from the mouth of the Lord.*" She asked Denise if they could discuss it in her coffee shop so her employees could listen in. Another believer later led her to the Lord and then she invited her mom to read the Bible with Denise as well.

The Greggs realized that God had already prepared people long before they arrived in the obscurity of Daiji. As Zach describes it, "You think about the glory of God and how He is working in so many different dimensions and people and aligning everything in His timing—it just blows my mind at how amazing He is." In His graciousness, God allowed the Greggs to be a part of a lot of stories in Daiji.

After two years as full-time language students, Zach and Denise finally felt ready to step into more direct ministry. They had always planned to move to an area north of Daiji with even less of a gospel witness. One of the challenges of the move would be arranging new visas. Most countries require foreigners to apply for permission to live within their borders for a particular reason, such as study or business.

Zach and Denise didn't realize that for more than a decade, the believing community in Daiji had been asking the Lord to place Christian teachers in the university where the Greggs had studied language. God chose to answer that prayer through Zach and Denise. The university leadership approached them and asked, "Would you stay and teach English here?"

Zach and Denise decided immediately to refuse the offer. While they might not have said it out loud, deep down they felt that to be real missionaries, they had to go to the hardest place and do the hardest thing. With a handful of believers in a city of 500,000, Daiji was unreached, but not as unreached as the villages to the north. Staying would be too easy. But as they prayed, Zach and Denise realized one of the main reasons they were refusing the teaching jobs was pride. They confessed that to the Lord, changed course and stayed.

It's hard to overstate the value of the work visas the university provided for Zach and Denise. They had respectable jobs, a reason to live in the city and a life that their friends and neighbors understood. They taught the English language and Western culture, and the university left the details of the curriculum up to them. A lesson about British landmarks, for example, provided an opportunity to tell historical stories with a gospel flair. Discussions about cultural values easily drifted into conversations about grace, forgiveness and eternity.

The Greggs even developed an unexpected relationship with Han, the police chief responsible for all the foreigners in Daiji. Zach first met him in the cafeteria of the police station and thought, "I don't have any reason to be afraid of this guy. We could even be friends." So, he asked for his phone number, and over time Han and his wife became close friends with the Greggs. The two couples had their first babies just two months apart. Zach and Denise welcomed little Joel into the world right there in Daiji. When both Joel and Han's daughter were almost a year old, Zach snapped a photo of Han with one baby on each knee and reading from the *Jesus Storybook Bible*. He texted it to Han. Two years later, Zach spotted that photo framed in Han's office at the police station.

In his role as police chief, Han had seen a difference between foreigners who talked about Jesus and those who did not. Local believers also had a solid testimony in the city. Han even told Zach, "Once I retire from being a policeman, then I'll become a Christian." His hesitation to make such a change any sooner was understandable. While in theory, individuals could believe what they wanted, in practice, the government and society severely penalized people based on their religious convictions. Han could lose his job and retirement benefits. He might not be able to get a loan for a car or an apartment. He would certainly lose the respect of his friends and would probably be cut off from his family. Han counted the cost of following Jesus and decided *Not now*.

The risks weren't as high for foreigners, but Zach and Denise knew that a few specific things could cause the government to revoke their right to live and work in Daiji. For example, they were not allowed to distribute religious literature or talk about faith with anyone under the age of 18. The Greggs never hid their faith or lied about their activities. They did take care not to share information that could cause trouble for themselves or others. With some coaching from experienced missionaries, they didn't find it very difficult.

In Western culture, we often feel that we have to answer every direct question directly. Anything else feels dishonest. But East Asian culture doesn't have that expectation. People commonly sidestep questions as a polite way to keep personal information private. So, when Han asked directly if the Greggs had been sent to East Asia by a mission organization, Zach reframed the question the way a local person might: "Well, if you're asking if I'm a Christian, you know I love Jesus. And if you're asking if I want people to know about Him, of course I do. He changed my life." Han probably knew the answer to his original question, but he didn't push Zach for a yes or a no.

For five years, Zach and Denise navigated the social and political currents of Daiji with relative ease. They had good relationships with the university, local government and police. None of their students ever complained about their professionalism in the classroom or expressed concern that class discussions often drifted to spiritual topics. During that time, Denise gave birth to their second child, a daughter. The Greggs became team leaders and welcomed new missionaries who shared their love for the community and longed to see the people know and follow Jesus. Missionary life was playing out in much the way Zach and Denise had hoped—it was hard but worthwhile. They didn't realize that their journey with God would lead them to more than one precipice, and they would have to keep deciding whether to step off.

All in, From Billboard to Precipice

Zach & Denise Gregg's Story
Part 2

FORESHADOWING

The Greggs were well-established in Daiji and enjoying ministry, work and relationships when the political winds in East Asia began to shift. Zach and Denise started hearing about missionaries in other parts of the country having a hard time renewing their visas. Some were interrogated about their connections to other foreigners. The police confiscated and searched their phones and computers. Some were deported with little notice. Zach and Denise updated their contingency plans and waited. Denise frequently asked herself, *Is today the day the police are showing up at our door? Will I be asked questions? Will our kids see that?* One day at the peak of the tension, Zach noticed police cars in front of the university administration building as he walked to class, and he wondered, *Are they here for me?*

But the police didn't come for them, not then or ever. As days and then weeks passed without incident, the Greggs relaxed. It seemed that the obscurity of Daiji had protected them from scrutiny. *We're in the forgotten province,* Denise comforted herself. *We're going to be fine.* Zach and Denise had a new work contract with the university and valid visas. In the last week of July, they headed to the U.S. for a few months to deliver their third baby. They walked out of their apartment with four carry-ons and one large suitcase.

As the Greggs loaded a friend's car for the drive to the train station, Zach had an impulse to run back upstairs and grab a few more things. He says it must have been the Lord prompting him because he is not a planner or a detail guy. Zach pulled out their original marriage license, diplomas and the kids' birth certificates and grabbed a pair of sentimental Christmas stockings. He shoved it all into their suitcase and the Greggs started the long journey around the world with every intention to come back.

THE POINT OF NO RETURN

Once they settled in the U.S., Zach and Denise heard a fuller story of what was happening politically in East Asia and their uneasiness returned. *Maybe we're not forgotten after all.* A few months later, they received a phone call from a teammate who had just returned to Daiji after a visit to her home country. She told them she had walked into her Daiji apartment, travel-weary and jetlagged, to find it completely ransacked. The police were waiting, and they interrogated her for the next 15 hours. They gained access to files on her computer that directly implicated Zach and Denise as missionaries and team leaders. Then they gave her 72 hours to leave the country.

That phone call set off a flurry of communication, prayer and decision-making. The Greggs conferred with their mission agency leadership and asked, *What's the best way we can love everybody even if it's the hard thing?* If the government had identified Zach and

Denise as missionaries, they were confident police would soon be knocking at their teammates' doors. To minimize the danger to local believers, the whole team would have to leave—and quickly. Zach and Denise called each family, one after another, and gave them three days to pack up, say what goodbyes they could and leave East Asia permanently. "I know this is like a gut shot," Zach told them, "But we really feel it's the best move."

The hardest part of those three days for Zach was not being with his team during the crisis. It went against everything he believed about leadership. His team was in trouble, but he could only watch from the other side of the world. He talked to Denise about flying back to help the others evacuate, but they didn't know if he'd be allowed in and decided not to risk drawing attention to their friends in Daiji.

The Greggs' teammates insisted on going to their apartment to retrieve a few special items for them, but Zach and Denise struggled with what to ask for. The things they wanted most wouldn't fit in a suitcase, like a crib Zach had built for Joel when he was a baby. In the end, they settled on a book and stuffed animal for each of the kids—Winnie-the-Pooh and Minnie Mouse—and sentimental mugs for Zach and Denise. The team said a few goodbyes in Daiji and then dispersed to their home countries.

Just like that, Zach and Denise's all-in, long-haul ministry in East Asia was over.

GRIEVING

When the crisis of the evacuation passed, Zach and Denise began to process the finality of their departure. For a while they kept asking each other, *Can we really not go back?* Sometimes Zach would say, "Maybe I'll just try," and Denise would caution him, "I don't know if that's a good idea. You have three kids now." And then another day she'd tell him, "Maybe you should try."

The Greggs had struggled through phases of confusion and frustration in Daiji until they grew to love the city in all its mixed-up eccentricity. Now they grieved the sudden loss of relationships with teachers, neighbors, friends, shopkeepers and students. They wanted their friends in Daiji to know they didn't just abandon them. Everyone had expected them to come back with a new baby.

Zach and Denise's family and friends in Georgia hurt for them and tried to understand their grief. "It's like you had a house fire and lost everything," people said. And in a way that was true. "We did lose sentimental things," Zach acknowledges, "but it was more an abrupt end to a season of life where God did so much in our hearts. What do we do with that?" If your house burns down, you don't also lose dozens of relationships and all the familiar landmarks of your life. The Greggs lost all of that and didn't even get to say goodbye. Denise describes it as "a whole life that is dead now."

The Greggs' youngest children were too little to feel the losses, but Joel kept asking, "When are we going home?" He asked about his favorite stuffed animals and the students he had played with at the university in Daiji. He loved digging in the long-jump sand pit in the athletic complex and wanted to know when he could do that again. Zach and Denise had to tell him, "We don't think you're going to get to."

As disorienting as the sudden transition was for all of them, the Greggs saw God's graciousness in protecting them, especially the kids. Joel, now four, thought policemen and soldiers were the coolest thing ever. Denise is grateful he never had to see his dad arrested by scary men. His happy memories of Daiji weren't tarnished by fear or trauma related to their departure. He just didn't understand why they couldn't go home.

Besides the physical and relational losses, the Greggs also struggled with the loss of their ministry dreams. They were just finally hitting their stride in Daiji. After years of effort, they were proficient enough in the language to have deep spiritual conversations. More and more students were interested in reading the Bible and learning about Jesus.

As the start of the next semester approached, the dean of the university in Daiji texted Zach, *Where are you? What's going on?* Zach and Denise decided to just tell their friends that it was becoming harder for Americans to live in Daiji because of the strained relationship between their countries. Even Han, the police chief, seemed to be unaware of the crackdown on foreigners. It was probably conducted on a federal level, well above his pay grade. He still calls Zach every once in a while to share news from Daiji and ask when the Greggs are coming back.

Zach and Denise will probably never go back to Daiji. But they didn't stay in Georgia, either. God had a few more precipices for them to step off and plenty more surprises along the way.

RECALIBRATING

As some of the initial shock and grief of not being able to return to East Asia wore off, Zach and Denise looked at their options. Lots of options. Their sending church approached them about taking a position at the church. Zach looked for jobs and considered going back to school. The Greggs thought and prayed about each possibility, but ultimately set it aside. For them, the decision boiled down to *Where does God want us to follow Him?* While they felt confident to turn down each option, they also had a sense that time was running out.

Zach felt like a failure because he didn't know how to lead his family forward. They couldn't receive missionary support indefinitely without some clarity on their next ministry role.

All the while, Zach and Denise struggled to understand what their departure from East Asia meant in relation to their calling to missions. Had God closed the door completely? It felt like everyone's assumption before they left for the field had come true: They hadn't stayed for the long haul. The Greggs turned to Mark and Alice, who encouraged them, saying, "Don't forget your original calling." But Zach and Denise wondered, *What does it mean when that door is closed and locked and boarded up?*

As they wrestled through their grief and confusion, the Lord nudged the Greggs toward a next step through a series of unconnected conversations each suggesting they talk to the same church planter in New England. After the third nudge in less than a week, Zach told the Lord, *I'm a little thick-headed sometimes, but I hear You. I'll call him.* Denise listened in the background as Zach and the pastor had a long conversation, and by the time they hung up, she knew, *We're moving to New England.*

Through the process of considering and turning down job possibilities, the Greggs were still convinced, *Ministry to the unreached is absolutely where our hearts are.* That's why they had gone to Daiji and one reason it hurt so much to leave. They were surprised to hear that New England also had a huge spiritual need and very few gospel-teaching churches.

So, the Greggs made their next all-in decision. With the door back to Daiji solidly closed, they resigned from Pioneers, moved to New England and joined the staff of the young church plant. Even though Zach and Denise believed they were following the Lord, it felt like another loss. Pioneers was family, and leaving meant that door was really closed. Denise cried when they sent their resignation letter.

Just a few months after leaving almost everything they owned in Daiji, the Greggs pulled away from Georgia in a U-Haul full of household items donated by their friends and church family—couches, beds, a dining room set, a crib. One of Denise's college friends turned up at their door with a stack of towels, adding, "I got you gray because you have kids." Zach and Denise's new church family in New England rallied around them, listened to their stories from East Asia and let them continue to process the transition. The Greggs hadn't expected that their time there would be as much for their own processing and recovery as anything they could offer to the church. The pastor became like a brother to Zach, and Denise joined other women in a tight-knit accountability group. They both began to heal as they felt the Lord loving them through His Church. He gently provided what they needed even when they didn't know what that was.

RECONSIDERING

About six months after Zach and Denise moved to New England, they were invited to join a think tank about how to help the missionaries who had been displaced from East Asia re-engage with the unreached. Many of the participants had been through similar experiences. "It was encouraging to be with them," Zach remembers, "praying, dreaming and expecting God to work. It was powerful to see and be among those who the Spirit of God was pushing along to continue the race." Much to their surprise, Zach and Denise felt the Lord rekindling their desire to continue the race.

Denise describes their first nudges back to the field as an initial *Well, maybe.* "We had walked through the process of grieving and were getting to a point where we could sense the Lord still calling us," Zach explains. The Greggs found themselves perpetually drawn to their town's international markets and neighborhoods, always on the lookout for immigrants or refugees to befriend. They realized their hearts were wired to seek out cross-cultural relationships.

And the Greggs weren't the only ones lifting their eyes to the wider world. Zach's role at the church included teaching about the needs of the global Church and encouraging prayer for the unreached. When he shared with the elders that he and Denise were considering another cross-cultural role, they were surprised but supportive. The young church had never sent a missionary to the field before. While Zach and Denise would be sorely missed, they saw the opportunity to send a family who had become one of their own as an exciting new challenge.

A few months later, the missions pastor at one of the Greggs' supporting churches in Georgia called with some news. "I think God is raising up a team of people from this church to go overseas. They could use someone with experience to lead them. Would you pray about it?" The Georgia church had decided to focus its mission efforts on the people group the Greggs had originally planned to work among in East Asia before they heard about the unengaged groups near Daiji. Zach was ready to consider anything. Denise wasn't as open. She felt like they'd "been there, tried that." But they did pray, inviting Mark and Alice and others to join them, and after a month they both felt the Lord confirm His calling to lead the team. With East Asia closed to them, they decided to reach a large cluster of the church's focus people group who live in Central Asia.

The Greggs' church in Georgia agreed that this time the Greggs would formally be sent out by their new church in New England since they had never sent a missionary before. To Zach and Denise, it felt like jumping into the river of what God was already doing among their partner churches. And they jumped in deep. To minister effectively to their focus people group, they expected to have to learn three more languages. They would face a new wave of culture shock and begin building a network of relationships from scratch. Much more aware of the cost this time than when they first went to the field, the Greggs re-joined Pioneers and moved back to Georgia temporarily with the expectation of leaving for Central Asia two months later. That was the spring of 2020.

ALL-IN AGAIN

The Greggs and their team were stuck in Georgia for 14 months. COVID-19 restrictions shut down visa processing, universities and businesses across Central Asia. Zach and Denise remember that year of waiting as one of the toughest of their lives. They lived with constant ambiguity, having no idea when borders would reopen. They questioned everything. *What are we doing? When are we going to get there? Are we going to get there?*

Their team hung on as they tried one entry strategy after another. Originally, they wanted to go as English teachers. They were told they could only teach online from the U.S., and their classes would be in the middle of the night, Georgia time. Then they tried to go as students, but the government was not issuing student visas. Out of desperation, Zach and Denise eventually applied for a business visa.

Their visas were granted in July 2021 and within weeks they were on a plane to their new home in Central Asia. Remembering some of the hard lessons from their arrival in Daiji, Zach sent Denise out on the second day to buy kitchen supplies and pillows for the house. They had just 30 days to legally register a business, and they made it—just barely.

Although most of the people group Zach and Denise desire to

serve have lived in the region for generations, they have never really had a homeland. The two dominant regional powers have each attempted to eradicate their language and culture. No country fully claims them. They are a minority everywhere.

Zach and Denise understand that persistent sense of un-rooted-ness at some level, although the reasons are different. In 10 years of marriage, the Greggs lived in 13 homes. Their choices impact their kids as well. Moving to Central Asia triggered a new stage of processing for Joel. For nearly a year he told everyone, "I'm from Asia." He's not wrong, and thanks to his dad's last-minute packing addition, he has a birth certificate to prove it.

Whether they realized it or not, Zach and Denise chose a life of perpetual transition and uncertainty when they answered God's call to serve the unreached. The experience has changed Zach's under-standing of faithfulness and perseverance. "Before going to East Asia, I felt like it was my responsibility to stick it out when things got hard. I looked up to the generation of missionaries before us who perse-vered and stayed on the field. But I've learned that it's not always up to us. For me, now, it's not so much the length of time, the people I serve with, even what I'm doing on the field. I've been reminded that this journey is about being *with* the Lord, and when you are confused or hurting, to be real with the Body and let the Body do what God's made it to do."

Zach and Denise are still all-in people. They've just broadened their definition of what giving their *all* includes, and the number of places they may invest *in*. They learned that faithfulness doesn't always mean digging in and staying on. Sometimes it means stepping back and starting over. Following God rarely takes us where we expect, and even when it does, He doesn't necessarily keep us there for long.

Lands of Milk & Honey

Frank & Eileen Goodman's Story
Part 1

ANYWHERE BUT THERE

Frank and Eileen Goodman arrived at an orientation for new missionaries near the end of 2001 with a lot of enthusiasm and only one stipulation: "We'll go anywhere except to a Muslim country." Eileen had worked for Muslim men once and their view and treatment of women had grated on her. Frank shared her frustration, and neither of them wanted to repeat that experience. They were also living in the immediate aftermath of the 9/11 attacks on New York, and the Muslim world felt more threatening than ever before. The Goodmans were willing to go anywhere else.

Frank had started his career as an engineer. He worked on government contracts and was used to following instructions. He came to orientation with the attitude, *Just tell us where to go.* But to his surprise, "That's not the way Pioneers rolls." Instead of handing out assignments to fill vacancies, their interview team asked about their gifts, strengths and sense of leading from God. Frank and Eileen didn't feel that the Lord had directed them anywhere in particular, except to somewhere that wasn't Muslim. That was Monday.

On Wednesday, the Goodmans mentioned in a casual conversation that it would be nice to serve somewhere Frank could use his engineering and management experience. A mission leader responded with an idea that defined the next two decades (and counting) of their lives: "Why don't you go to the Kaumi of South Asia?"

By divinely ordained happenstance, Eileen had spent a semester in college researching the lives of Kaumi women. "They grabbed my heart like none other," she says, "but I never thought about being called to their country." The Goodmans knew that the Kaumi were nearly 100 percent Muslim and their homeland had been wracked by decades of violence, insurrection and corruption. But somehow, while Muslims, in general, seemed intimidating and inhospitable to the Goodmans, the Kaumi people, specifically, did not. The need for humanitarian and development work in the region meant engineers and project managers were in high demand. Frank would be able to be a blessing to the community in both physical and spiritual ways.

"Immediately, the idea grabbed us both," Frank remembers. Eileen describes it as "a divine moment that we were able to set aside our personal requirements and say, *This is holy. This is something we need to obey.*" They both mentally committed, on the spot, to serving in South Asia among the Kaumi.

COUNTING THE COST

The first few weeks after orientation, as the Goodmans started telling their friends and family they planned to serve among the Kaumi, they received a lot of confirmation. When Eileen's dad first heard where they were going, he told his wife, "I would have been surprised if they had said anything else!" Frank remembers thinking, *This feels like a yellow brick road. Everything is just lining up.*

But not everyone thought it was a good idea to move so close to a major conflict zone right after 9/11. A third of the world's Muslims live in South Asia. When the Goodmans told a friend in the military their plans, he burst out laughing. Eventually, he noticed Frank and Eileen weren't laughing with him and asked in shock, "Are you serious?!" Frank jokes they were the first missionaries Pioneers ever received hate mail about. It wasn't really hate mail, but two or three people did write to say sending a young family to such an unstable area would be a terrible mistake. Eileen gave birth to their first child, Madison, eight months before the Goodmans left for the field.

Frank and Eileen were theoretically aware of the risks when they agreed to move to a volatile area, but as they prepared for departure, the theory became much more real. The agency asked them to prepare a will, provide dental records and identify who should take custody of Madison if they were both killed or kidnapped. "It was very sobering," Eileen remembers. "We had to go in with our eyes wide open that we were potentially signing off on our own deaths." While the reality of risk added weight to their departure, it didn't deter them. Both Frank and Eileen were raised on biographies of missionaries who set out with their belongings packed in coffins and did not expect to return to their home countries.

The Lord used Bible passages about God's people entering the Promised Land to reassure Eileen about taking her baby to South Asia. She felt Him saying, *This is going to be your Promised Land, and if you don't go because you're scared of the giants, you're going to miss out.* She wondered, *Lord, are we talking about the same place? Is it really going to be my land filled with milk and honey?* It didn't seem possible. But looking back now, she says that's exactly what it turned out to be.

MAKING A LIFE

The Goodmans never expected to stay in South Asia forever. Although Madison was only an infant, Frank and Eileen already anticipated that they would probably not be able to meet her educational and social needs through high school in the Kaumi region of South Asia. "We were there for the long-ish haul," Frank says, "maybe 15 years." Still, they jumped in with a long-term mindset. A lot can happen in 15 years.

After six months of language school in the capital, the Goodmans moved to the town of Iman, which sits in a seasonal floodplain. A satellite view gives the impression that a river of sand has burst through a mountain gorge and threatens to inundate Iman's outlying neighborhoods with rippling dunes. The gridded neighborhoods appear orderly, if monochromatic. The image was taken in the dry season, and from a few thousand feet above the town, every green tree stands out individually against a beige backdrop.

Eileen was surprised by how quickly she began to feel comfortable in a country that had once felt so foreign and intimidating. As she learned the language and developed relationships, she started to see why God had called her, in particular, to minister to Kaumi people. She loved the honesty of her local friends and the relational emphasis in their communities. She admired their passion for hospitality and even grew to respect some aspects of Islam. She told the Lord, *This must be why you sent me to a Muslim community. I understand wanting to pass my faith on to my children. I understand wanting my faith to be part of every single thing in my life.*

But not everything about life in a conservative Muslim culture was easy for Eileen to accept. Dressing according to local standards became a constant source of frustration. Kaumi women were expected to cover completely from neck to ankle. Eileen constantly wondered, *Am I dressed appropriately? Am I covered enough?* In the early months, she doubted she would ever master the art of wearing a headscarf properly. Worse still, women's clothing was made from heavy fabric that didn't breathe well, and that made the hot season nearly unbearable. During a visit to the U.S., the Goodmans attended an outdoor funeral service in the summer. Frank looked around at all the men sweating in dark suit coats while the women chatted in cotton sundresses. *It's the opposite of Iman!* he thought. *This must be how Eileen feels all the time.*

For as long as she lived among the Kaumi, Eileen continued to wrestle with the tension between the mandates of local custom and her need for personal freedom. She told the Lord, *I know the cultural expectations and I'll play that game, but I don't want to lose myself and my heart in the process just to conform to others' standards.* Eventually, Eileen figured out compromises to make herself more comfortable while still being modest. For example, she had a traditional women's outfit made from the fabric usually used for men's clothing. It was much lighter and cooler.

SEEDS IN DESERT SOIL

The Goodmans knew from the start that ministry in South Asia would be hard, and measurable results would likely be scarce. They didn't expect to preach to enraptured crowds or baptize dozens of converts every Sunday. They *did* hope for spiritual fruit as they introduced people to Jesus, one by one or family by family. Early on, Eileen asked Frank, "What if we minister here for 15 years and nobody comes to faith?" He answered, "Even if it's just one person, it's still worth it." The impact of their ministry might not be obvious for years, or even generations, but God would cause the seeds of the gospel to eventually grow and bear fruit, even in the seeming spiritual desert of Iman.

Figuring out how they would go about planting those gospel seeds turned out to be a significant challenge for the Goodmans. As they finished full-time language study and transitioned into their long-term roles, they each had different expectations of what those roles would be. Eileen expected Frank to focus on the more obvious aspects of ministry—sharing the gospel with Kaumi men. Neither she nor Frank realized at first that he was better suited for humanitarian aid projects that benefited the people of Iman. He also loved discipleship, but there were almost no believers to disciple.

Of the two of them, Eileen was more drawn to overt ministry. At the time, they didn't find many models in the missions world of wives having the more prominent ministry role in families. They wondered, *Are we doing it wrong?* especially as they added another daughter and then a son to the family. Eileen says the key was learning to let go of her expectations of Frank and appreciate how God had made each of them. Over time, and with the support of their field leaders, they figured out a balance that allowed them each to serve in the ways they were gifted.

As the Goodmans settled into life among the Kaumi, Frank had an opportunity to put his management experience to good use as the director of a humanitarian project. Frank's job was to oversee logistics, finances and personnel. "It was really about managing the politics and preventing corruption," he explains. Serving the community in practical ways also provided informal opportunities to share the gospel with neighbors and co-workers. Frank's faith showed in his work, especially his honesty.

In Kaumi culture, people were not only willing to lie for various reasons but felt a *responsibility* to lie to protect themselves or others from embarrassment. Frank employed a driver to relieve some of the stress of navigating difficult roads. While the driver seemed to have a strong internal sense of integrity, he occasionally reported to Frank that he'd lied to someone on his behalf to cover over an awkward situation. Frank would always tell him, "You don't have to lie for me. I want to be honest in my work and my personal life." After many hours of conversation in the car over the years, the driver came to understand that Frank's integrity was rooted in his relationship with Christ.

Another Kaumi friend, a plumber who did several projects in the Goodmans' home, was injured in a motorcycle accident. Extended family members told him, "We're here for you!" But they weren't. They soon returned to their normal lives, and the plumber was stuck at home, unable to afford private medical care or pay the bribes necessary to receive good care from the public health system. One of Frank's co-workers was a nurse, and she arranged to come every day to change the bandages on his wounds. Frank couldn't help medically, but he visited and encouraged him as he recovered. The plumber later shared with Frank, "You guys don't lie. You tell the truth."

Years later, when the Goodmans were out of the country and there was significant unrest in Iman, many of their Kaumi friends called to ask for help immigrating to the U.S. They needed letters of reference and help with paperwork. The plumber made an international call just to tell Frank he was doing fine. It was a strange message, so different from all the other calls. Frank doesn't know for sure, but he wonders if there was more to it, and if, perhaps, the plumber meant that he had found peace in an eternal sense, even if his circumstances were anything but fine.

While Frank directed the humanitarian project, Eileen helped start a small business that employed Kaumi widows. As her kids got older, she also helped start a preschool and kindergarten and trained a local leadership team to run it. She loved her work and the impact she saw on the community, but sometimes she wished for a more direct ministry connection. In quiet moments she thought to herself, *Wouldn't it be amazing if I could manage a team like this, but it was for ministry?*

Eileen treasured her interactions with Kaumi women. One day, as she was praying about what relationships to focus on, she felt the Lord nudging her to visit a particular neighbor. She obediently went to the house and started chatting with a mother and daughter. Without any prompting, they suddenly announced, "We've seen a Jesus movie, and we love this Jesus person. Can you tell us more about Him?" Eileen was delighted to oblige them. Over several visits and conversations, they fell even more in love with Jesus and put their faith in Him. Eileen connected them with a group of believing Kaumi women who continued to disciple them.

Women also sought Eileen out to tell her about their dreams. One friend dreamed of a bright, bright light. A voice said, "I am the light of the world. Go call Eileen and she will tell you more about Me." The woman obeyed, and Eileen had a chance to explain to her who the light of the whole world is. "You can't make this stuff up!" Eileen laughs. "It was crazy! Those were sweet times because so much of life in South Asia was just waiting, being available and then journeying with people in the Scriptures when the opportunities came."

HANGING ON

The Goodmans believed God had brought them to Iman, but there were still times they each thought, *We're done.* South Asia is a hard place to live. The heat. The poverty. The oppressive aspects of Kaumi culture and Islam. Corruption. The constant threat, and often reality, of violence. Frank and Eileen felt the weight of it all, and at times they longed for an easier life.

The Kaumi people's homeland in South Asia simmered with tension between various political, religious and militia groups, all of them armed. Foreigners and local Christians were sometimes targeted. When several of Frank and Eileen's co-workers were killed in an extremist attack, the Goodmans reacted in very different ways. From Frank's perspective, the violence was contained in a remote area quite a distance away. While he mourned the loss of colleagues, he saw little connection to their family in Iman. Eileen, on the other hand, was ready to be done. She told Frank, "You're going to stick this out until there's a war right at our door." Something had to change.

The Goodmans returned to the U.S. and sought help at a debriefing program for missionaries. Through some extended conversations with counselors, they realized they were viewing the situation from different perspectives. Frank was evaluating the risks on a rational level. Eileen was in mom mode. They were able to sort through the facts and the emotions and together establish new thresholds that would indicate it was time to evacuate.

MOVING ON

When Frank and Eileen returned to the field a few months later, the security situation stabilized. Nevertheless, the Goodmans realized that their season of ministry in Iman was drawing to a close sooner than they had originally anticipated. They had always planned to leave South Asia when their kids were teenagers, but now felt their 15-year time frame had been overly optimistic. Madison, their oldest, was only nine, but according to Kaumi culture, she was just three years away from womanhood.

When Kaumi girls reach puberty, their freedoms come crashing down. Their entire lives become focused on protecting their marriage-ability and family honor. The only respectable places for a teenage girl to go are to school and the homes of relatives. That's it. Even a rumor of impurity can damage the family's reputation and deter suitors.

Madison wasn't Kaumi or in need of suiters, but she was beautiful and spoke Kaumi well. Frank and Eileen expected to have to navigate the cultural complexities of marriage proposals very soon. Madison's opportunities for social interaction were already restricted by both cultural expectations and safety measures. Kidnapping was still a concern. Constantly mitigating risks added another layer of stress to the whole family. Schooling options were limited, and there were no safe extracurricular activities except English classes, which felt rather pointless for a native speaker. With their leaders' support, Frank and Eileen decided to leave Iman in three years when Madison would turn 12.

Having years to plan their departure felt very strange in a country where so many foreign workers left suddenly and dramatically. The Goodmans had seen co-workers leave due to health crises, tragedies and violence, some after just a few years, others after decades of ministry. Closure was a rarity.

Frank and Eileen describe their departure as "the antithesis of evacuating." Eileen handed her ministry responsibilities over to capable Kaumi leaders. A new expat family arrived, and the husband took over Frank's management role at work. They lined up jobs for everyone who relied on them for an income and connected the small group of believers they were discipling with other Christians who could support them.

Frank says they had more closure than any of their peers who had left in the past. Eileen considers it a gift from the Lord. "Frank and I are both planners. God was very gracious to let us leave in an organized way." They flew out of Iman for the last time right on schedule, a few weeks before Madison's twelfth birthday. Frank had already declined several tentative marriage proposals on her behalf. The Goodmans say it wasn't hard to leave Iman when the time came. They were ready to go.

JUST ENOUGH MANNA

When Frank and Eileen first started planning their departure from South Asia, they discussed both staying in the U.S. and returning overseas to a different location. The needs of their kids were at the top of their priority list. Eileen's father had been a diplomat and her family moved every few years both in the U.S. and abroad. Frank's upbringing was the opposite. When he was five, his family moved a half-mile away from the house where his father was born and his parents still lived there. The stability and rootedness Frank enjoyed as a child had some advantages, but he wanted to continue raising their kids abroad. "We had so much more to offer them as people growing up overseas," he explains.

The Goodmans were concerned that living in the U.S. for a full year during the transition would indicate to their prayer and financial supporters that they were disengaging from ministry. They worried that people might question their commitment. So, even before leaving Iman, Frank and Eileen started researching other places they could live and minister to Kaumi people. Southern Europe quickly rose to the top of their list. Friends had recently relocated from Iman to a city on the Mediterranean coast and described it as an amazing place for ministry. Frank and Eileen visited them and realized that it was, truly, the next logical step. Large numbers of Kaumi refugees were transiting through the port or settling in town, and many of them were open to the gospel. Outside the social and political pressures of their homeland, they had more freedom to investigate the teachings of Jesus. Another perk of ministry in Europe was that Frank and Eileen wouldn't necessarily have to learn another language. In many Mediterranean cities, they could get by with English.

During the year the Goodmans spent connecting with prayer and financial partners in the U.S., moving to southern Europe remained the leading option. But life in America had its draws as well. The kids attended public school for the first time and loved it. They were getting a good education and making friends. Madison met a Kaumi family in Walmart and soon Eileen was engaged in a burgeoning ministry with a small community of refugees.

Frank and Eileen were also very, very tired. The stress of 11 years in South Asia had worn them down. Frank's blood pressure was always significantly higher in Iman than in the U.S. He admits, "There were definitely some signs of us having been there maybe too long." Eileen remembers, "Just the thought of living there again made me tired." When the cultural and security pressures they had lived under for more than a decade dissipated, they both began to relax.

As the Goodmans became more and more comfortable with suburban American life, the idea of returning to cross-cultural ministry—even somewhere less intense—felt more and more daunting. Eileen remembers grumbling to the Lord about how amazing America was and how isolating life in Europe would be for the kids. She dreaded homeschooling, especially after they'd had such a good year of classroom interaction. Did they really have to leave?

As the temptation to give up on missions and stay home grew, the Lord brought the story of His provision of manna for the Israelites to Eileen's attention in a fresh way. While the manna was a wonderful blessing, if they gathered more than they needed for the day, the leftovers would rot and be infested with maggots. Eileen felt the Lord gently chiding her, *This year is a good gift for your family, but you've gathered enough. If you overstay your welcome, it's going to turn sour. This is not what I have for you.* That was all the reminder Eileen needed. She realized *I don't want maggots. Let's go!* At the end of the year, the Goodmans packed up again, said goodbye and launched into a new season of life and ministry on the Mediterranean coast. "I'm so glad we did," Eileen says now. "It's been very rich."

Lands of Milk & Honey

Frank & Eileen Goodman's Story
Part 2

A KID'S-EYE VIEW

Despite the challenges, dangers and stressors, Frank and Eileen summarize their experience in South Asia like this: "Our life was rich, especially our family life." Eileen adds, "When our kids go through hard times, we're always checking in with one another. 'Is everybody okay here? Do we all feel like this is where God has called us?'" Serving as a family has always been the Goodmans' priority, and even though their kids are now older, they still emphasize that mindset, challenging them, "You need to find a place to serve. This is what we do."

Each of the Goodman kids processed the transitions from South Asia to the U.S. to Europe in his or her own way. Madison is grateful they left Iman when they did. She was ready to be done with the ever-increasing limitations on where she could go, what she could wear and who she could talk to. She also says Iman was a really good place to grow up. She's now launching into adulthood and Frank and

Eileen are delighted to see her pursuing ministry among refugees on her own initiative.

The Goodmans' younger daughter, Laura, struggled more with the move to the U.S. She complained to her parents, "Iman was so much safer than America." That may be because when they were in South Asia, the Goodmans constantly mitigated security risks. That lifestyle felt normal and safe to her. Like most people in Iman, the Goodmans had walls around their yard and an unarmed security guard on duty all day and night. He served as a sort of bouncer, screening visitors at the gate.

Fortunately, the house the Goodmans moved into in the U.S. had a fenced-in front yard, but it was nowhere near as imposing as their concrete block wall in Iman. Visitors could open the gate and walk right up to the front door. Laura felt exposed and unsafe for the first few months. Over time, she adjusted and even enjoyed aspects of life in the U.S., but when they landed in Europe she told her parents, "It's so good to be back in Asia." Laura knew they weren't technically in Asia, but the atmosphere felt familiar. Frank and Eileen are grateful that all three of their kids still speak fondly of Iman. All of them want to go back to visit, especially the oldest two who have more memories there.

STARTING OVER

The Goodmans arrived on the Mediterranean coast in the summer of 2015. Eileen describes the transition as "lots of stresses and firsts." For two months they lived in a tiny apartment overlooking a run-down neighborhood. Madison and Laura shared a bed and Ryan, the youngest, slept on the couch. They didn't have a car. Eileen had been dreading homeschooling but got started with it. Madison struggled with the transition to an online curriculum. She missed the interaction and friendships of her school in the States. Ryan often cried, missing his cousins, friends he had made in the U.S. and the toys he left behind.

It hurt Eileen to watch her kids struggle. She wondered, *Can I trust the Lord with their hearts?* Over time, though, everyone adjusted. Homeschooling wasn't as bad as Eileen had feared. The kids' desire to make friends drove them to work hard at learning the local language and soon they were busy with hobbies and social activities. Frank had an easier time settling in than the rest of the family. Just a few days after arriving, he started an English-language MBA program at a public university. The classes provided an opportunity to learn some local culture and build relationships with staff and other students.

After a few months, the Goodmans moved to a nicer apartment. Eileen started to enjoy that she could blend in much more in Europe than in South Asia. She could wear what she wanted, go where she wanted and talk to anyone she could manage to communicate with through English, Kaumi or snippets of the local language. She remembers, "It was nice to not have to worry about adapting to the culture every time I stepped out the door."

The Goodmans were also excited to discover that the Lord had moved several missionary families they knew from South Asia to the same city in Europe that summer. "It was like being with extended family," Eileen explains, "because we had so many shared experiences." The Goodmans had been planning the transition for years with no idea that southern Europe would become the epicenter of a massive refugee crisis the summer they arrived. In 2015, almost a million migrants poured into Europe, fleeing war and persecution in North Africa, the Middle East and South Asia. Many arrived in coastal cities by boat and many of them were Kaumi. Eileen points out, "God had a number of us in place to help receive them. I thought, *Look at You, Lord. You're so good at being prepared.*"

Within days of the Goodmans' arrival, word spread through the missionary and refugee communities that a Kaumi speaker with ministry experience had arrived and was available to help. Eileen found herself inundated with invitations to lead Bible studies and run programs for refugees. "We saw God using the decade we spent in Iman to open doors in Europe," she remembers. "It gave us credibility. That was encouraging."

LINGUA(S) FRANCA

One of the factors that attracted the Goodmans to Europe was that they could jump into ministry with Kaumi refugees without having to learn a new language first. Many residents of their city spoke English, which meant Frank and Eileen could function right from the beginning. They both wanted to reach at least a base level in the local language but didn't anticipate spending a lot of time on it. Frank had always found the Kaumi language to be a struggle. He had been able to manage the humanitarian project in Iman because the staff adapted to his vocabulary, but he never felt completely comfortable in extended conversations. Eileen reached a high fluency in Kaumi, but they both hit an unexpected language wall in Europe: They weren't just working with Kaumi people.

A lot of the South Asian refugees streaming into their city in 2015 were from a culturally and linguistically similar but distinct people group called the Mobarek. If you picture the Indo-Persian language family of South Asia as a tree, Kaumi and Mobarek are closely related branches. The basic grammatical structure is the same, but a lot of vocabulary differs because each branch incorporates loan words from different source languages. Kaumi speakers usually understand

Mobarek, but to Mobarek speakers, Kaumi sounds awkward, almost like Shakespearean English to an American.

For their first few years in Europe, Frank and Eileen intentionally focused on increasing their Mobarek comprehension and vocabulary, mainly by listening to podcasts, sermons and other recordings. Frank now finds it easier to follow conversations in Mobarek than in Kaumi. God even used Frank and Eileen to help bridge the language and cultural gaps between Mobarek and Kaumi friends who didn't always have the patience to understand one another. "It's just been really sweet to be a part of that process," Eileen says.

The unexpected effort required to function in Mobarek limited Frank and Eileen's ability to pursue the local European language, but they slowly chipped away at it. "Our heads felt like they were exploding a bit," Eileen remembers.

FINDING A FIT

Having learned from their experience in Iman, Frank and Eileen now approached their life in Europe with an attitude of facilitating each other's individual ministry visions. In addition to his graduate studies, Frank became the finance director of a humanitarian aid organization that served a large refugee camp. On a single day at the peak of the migrant crisis, more than 10,000 people made the dangerous journey across the Mediterranean from Turkey and North Africa. They arrived in overcrowded rubber rafts to seek asylum in the European Union. The rafts were designed to hold about 15 people, but smugglers often loaded as many as 50. And that was after many of them had endured a difficult journey by land from South Asia.

In his role as finance director, Frank mainly worked from an office in the city rather than directly with refugees, but he visited the camp occasionally. Near the end of 2015, he went out to help clean the reception center where boats carrying refugees first landed. The center was just a chain-link fence and a few tents designed to corral people in orderly lines while they waited to board buses to the main camp.

As Frank cleaned and organized the area, a single rubber raft with an outboard motor landed on the rocky beach. About 20 people were aboard. The weather had been terrible and hardly anyone attempted the crossing that day. Suddenly, Frank recognized one of the new arrivals as part of the facilities staff at the office he had managed in Iman. Frank called his name and soon found himself hugging the young man. "It was kind of weird," he says, "because we weren't close friends. And it was shocking to see him as a refugee." The Goodmans kept in touch and heard that he eventually settled in Germany.

DREAMS DO COME TRUE

While Frank spent the majority of his time focusing on humanitarian work, Eileen poured herself into leadership training to empower South Asian believers—both Kaumi and Mobarek—to plant churches and start multiplying Bible studies. In South Asia, small groups of believers struggled just to survive and they shared the gospel in their communities at great risk. But Europe was home to many Mobarek and Kaumi Christians, and they faced far less opposition to reaching and discipling their own people than they had in their homelands. Eileen celebrated that the believing refugee community was strong enough that she could play a supporting role. She remembered her longing back in Iman: *Wouldn't it be wonderful if I could do ministry-focused leadership training for women?* In southern Europe, she did exactly that. "So many dreams have come true for ministry here," she says.

Eileen also taught English classes to help newly arrived refugees integrate into European society. English skills helped them find jobs wherever they eventually settled. One day, Eileen walked into class and a student excitedly announced, "I met Marzia, who used to work for you in Iman." Eileen peppered him with questions and showed him a picture of Marzia to verify it was her friend. Eileen had wondered if she might turn up because she had always longed for a better life and had the kind of courage it takes to make it along the refugee corridor from South Asia to Europe.

Marzia had been looking for Eileen, too. She and her kids fled Iman when her abusive husband, who had abandoned them and taken a second wife, returned to try to take the children to an extremist school. She was asking every American she met if they knew the Goodmans. Eileen was thrilled when they finally reconnected and considered it a precious gift to have a friend in Europe she had known for more than a decade. At the same time, it was hard to see Marzia and her children struggling.

Many of the women Eileen ministered to fled their homelands not because of bombs and bullets, but to escape husbands who beat them and tried to sell their daughters as child brides. The mothers, powerless under Islamic law and a broken legal system, ran toward hope in Europe. The school where Eileen taught had to hire teachers for what they called "pre-beginner" classes. Many of the women who were trying to learn English so they could get jobs in Europe were illiterate in any language. One of the volunteers' eyes widened when Eileen explained that she would have to teach adults how to hold a pencil.

Just as in Iman, God sometimes spoke to refugee women through dreams. One day, as Eileen led a discussion group for South Asian refugees interested in learning about Jesus, a woman stood up and announced, "I am a Muslim, but I come to these classes to learn about the Holy Book. I had a dream and Mary and Jesus appeared to me. Jesus was dressed in white, and Mary told me to tell you that everything these people are telling and teaching us is true." Then she plopped back down in her seat. Eileen knew the village in South Asia where she and her family, none of whom were yet believers, used to live. Years earlier, all the missionaries in that area had to leave due to security concerns. They couldn't have guessed where and how the Lord would continue to work in the lives of people they had tried to reach.

As with the missionary community, Eileen found that her experience in South Asia opened doors and established credibility with refugees. She explains, "So many times I'll introduce myself when I'm teaching and share how much we love the Kaumi people and loved raising our kids in their homeland. Later on in the conversation, they'll be talking about trauma or pain or sadness, and they'll look directly at me and say, 'You understand. You were there.'"

Eileen couldn't always relate to their trauma, but she identified on a deep level with anything related to Kaumi culture. "It's a heart connection and it takes down walls," she says. "They just break out in smiles when I talk about how much our family loved life in Iman, especially the food. And then they start bringing me food, which I love. Out of their nothingness, they want to bless us."

Frank and Eileen saw so much value in having people with experience in South Asia serving refugees in Europe that they lobbied their regional leader to designate their city as a "strategic waiting place" for the missionaries still working in Iman. Should it be necessary for the team to pull out of South Asia, the Goodmans volunteered to help plug them into ministry among Kaumi refugees in Europe, either temporarily or long-term.

A DIFFERENT KIND OF FAITHFULNESS

"Ministry here is just fun," Eileen says. "That makes faithfulness and perseverance a lot easier." Frank points out that South Asia required a different kind of faithfulness. "We all pray that God would use us for His purposes and glory. Sometimes we have grand images of what that will be like. Yet when He selects us for the nitty-gritty, quiet or behind-the-scenes work, do we willingly accept the challenge of faithful obscurity?" In Iman, the Goodmans had to be faithful in an ambiguous and constantly changing ministry situation. There were no local churches to partner with. Church planting looked different than they imagined because new believers faced persecution.

Over time, Frank learned to be patient, to take advantage of every small opportunity and to prioritize humanitarian projects as meaningful ministry in their own right. That experience shaped the way he approaches ministry now in Europe. "During our time in Iman, God led me to see that part of my being faithful to His work is to be involved in the humanitarian side, even if there isn't a lot of opportunity to share my faith or do biblical discipleship."

In whatever circumstances Frank and Eileen find themselves, now or in the future, the one thing they count on to never change is the faithfulness of God. "Our perseverance comes from the Lord," Eileen emphasizes. "He gives us the strength to keep on going—the energy, the focus, the drive and the inspiration. Any faithfulness we have comes out of that strength."

Lands of Tea & Opportunity

Kristi Reid's Story

Part 1

CLARITY IN CHAOS

Kristi finished her fourth cup of tea with Jamila just as Jamila's children arrived home from school and the small apartment descended into mayhem. Jamila and her seven kids—including two sets of twins—had recently immigrated to the U.S. from South Asia. They and several other Kaumi families lived in Kristi's apartment complex. Kristi stopped by a few times a week to tutor Jamila in English, and it almost always ended in chaos.

When the kids arrived, they knocked over teacups, crunched the last of the cookies into the rug and scattered their mom's language notes. English class was over. But as Kristi stood up to say goodbye that afternoon, Jamila grabbed her arm. Her headscarf slipped down onto her shoulders and her eyes filled with tears. "Kristi," she said, "I'm so scared."

Shocked by Jamila's sudden intensity, Kristi asked, "What's going on?"

"I'm so afraid of going to hell. I think about it all the time and I can't sleep at night."

Right there, with one set of twins jumping on the couch and the other practicing martial arts on each other, Kristi had a chance to share her testimony and pray for her friend. She says Jamila was ready to hear some parts of the gospel and not others. They would have many more conversations about spiritual things in the future, but that chaotic afternoon proved pivotal for Kristi. She looked into Jamila's eyes and thought, *We're so different in almost every way. We follow different religions. She's married with seven kids. I'm single. She's way outside her home country. I've lived here my entire life. And yet we have feared some of the same things.*

That day, Kristi realized that her Kaumi neighbors had become real people to her—actual friends, not just "people over there who don't know Jesus." It was also the day she started to seriously consider whether God might want *her*, specifically, to take the gospel to Kaumi women. *He used me in this situation,* she marveled to herself, *God coordinated this moment and gave me something to share.*

WHO, ME?

Kristi grew up with a very specific and very scary image of missions. Missionaries were called by God to go somewhere unreached and far away and stayed there until they died. Kristi respected them for it, but she didn't identify with them. In her mind, long-term missions meant forever, and as a self-described homebody, she wasn't interested in leaving home forever.

Kristi also wasn't interested in raising support. *Ask people for money? Are you kidding?* She doesn't consider herself adventurous and is not the kind of person she thought missionaries were like. *I'm not a Bible teacher. Or a businessperson. I'm not super outgoing or charismatic or a natural leader. What on earth do I have to offer?* Moving away from family was probably her biggest barrier. Kristi is very close with her parents and sisters. She wrestled with God for months before finally accepting, *You know what? God can take care of my family without me. And He can take care of me without my family, too.*

Kristi was a teacher by profession, although she preferred tutoring to classroom instruction. Even before she became interested in missions, she thought she might teach English for a few years over-seas and pictured herself being an intentional witness for Christ while getting paid to do a job she enjoyed. To prepare for the possi-bility, she signed up for a cross-cultural training program that placed her in Jamila's neighborhood. Part-way through the program, Kristi's conversation with Jamila about fear helped her realize that she didn't just want to spend a few years teaching English. She wanted to bring the gospel to Kaumi people, maybe not forever, but for the long haul.

Kristi's decision to dedicate herself to ministry in South Asia elicited a lot of crazy looks. Most of her friends didn't know any missionaries and her church didn't talk about it much. "It was a huge privilege to get to be the one to open people's eyes to what God is doing around the world," she remembers, "but it was not normal." A lot of people were concerned about her, asking, "Are you going to be safe? There's no one to take care of you." Some people's very first response when she shared her desire to be a missionary was "I'll pray for a spouse for you." Kristi had mixed feelings about that. "Half of me was like, *Yes, please do pray.* The other half wondered, *What's wrong with going like I am?*"

Kristi didn't initially think that pursuing missions meant she was giving up on marriage. Once she learned that single women outnumber single men on the mission field about five to one, however, she realized, *Maybe I kind of am.* She describes it as "a moment of surrender for me to decide that finding a spouse was not the priority. It might happen, but everything else couldn't wait. I knew God was calling me to explore going with Him to a different part of the world. I couldn't spend time and energy on finding a relationship and pursuing missions at the same time."

NOT THE ONLY CRAZY ONE

Kristi's decision to leave marriage up to God and become a missionary still didn't make it easy to think about moving across the world alone. Some people voiced legitimate concerns about her ability to minister effectively to conservative Muslim people. "There's no place for single women in Islam," Kristi explains. People warned her, "They won't understand you. You should go somewhere you can do more as a single woman."

That's one reason she felt such relief when she came to Pioneers orientation. She says she approached the week "scared, but serious. As soon as I got into the missions bubble, though, everybody understood. I wasn't weird anymore. I might still be crazy, but at least I'm not the only one." Meeting people further along on the journey and discovering the resources available to help calmed her heart. *These are my people!* she thought. She met other singles who had served among unreached people groups all over the world. Best of all, Kristi enjoyed having people respond to her story with, "I think God is speaking to you" rather than, "Are you crazy? Are you sure?"

KEEPING OPTIONS OPEN

When it came right down to it, Kristi *wasn't* sure about serving God long-term in South Asia. The calling she felt was to the Kaumi people, not a particular location. But to minister effectively, she knew she needed to dive deep into the Kaumi language and culture. The best place to do that was in their homeland, even though it was a hard place to live and security risks were high. Meeting other people on a similar journey helped Kristi feel a little less crazy for pursuing that dream. But she also knew it might not work out.

After orientation, Kristi connected with Theresa, a leader who oversaw teams across several countries in South Asia. Theresa tried to coordinate a survey trip for Kristi, but months ticked by as she waited for a time when the team working among the Kaumi had the capacity to host her and the security situation was calm enough for visitors. As Kristi waited, she started raising her financial support and considered backup options. "Both my pre-field coach and the team in South Asia were very cautious. They didn't say no, but made it clear, 'This is a very hard part of the world. You might not be able to stay.'"

Kristi started contacting teams working with Kaumi people in other places, including U.S. cities, and had a video call with the Goodmans in Europe. She still wanted to start in South Asia, but followed the advice she kept hearing: "Consider all your options so that if you can't go or you get kicked out, you'll know people in other places." The wisdom of that strategy became clear when the COVID-19 pandemic stranded many missionaries in places they hadn't expected to be and kept missionaries-in-process, like Kristi, from going to their intended destinations as planned. Her survey trip to South Asia was postponed indefinitely.

Theresa and Kristi's pre-field coach at Pioneers helped her work out an arrangement with a team ministering to South Asian immigrants in the U.S. They welcomed Kristi to join them temporarily. "God had many lessons to teach me during that time," Kristi remembers. "Unknowns are not the easiest for me. There was a lot to learn." Everyone involved accepted the open-ended, unpredictable situation.

The team connected Kristi with Kaumi people in the city and with missionaries who had experience in the Indo-Persian world.

Kristi participated in some of the team's ministries, including teaching several Kaumi women to drive, which she describes as both terrifying and rewarding. But she spent the majority of her time studying the language. Her friendship with Jamila the year before had been based in English. Now it was time to learn Kaumi. "It's so hard to learn a language in an English-speaking place," Kristi says with a grimace, "and I didn't have a trained teacher."

Her temporary team connected her with Taara, a lovely Kaumi woman who spoke no English. Kristi spoke no Kaumi. That made communication hard even before Kristi discovered that Taara had never learned to read in any language. "Interacting with anything on paper was difficult," Kristi explains. Her curriculum used line drawings to learn basic vocabulary, but Taara wasn't used to interpreting pictures. She recognized objects in realistic photos printed in color, but the black-and-white images on Kristi's worksheets were just scribbles to her. So, Kristi had to switch to three-dimensional props. One day she brought a bag of fruits and vegetables to Taara's house and spent an afternoon pointing at them and repeating their names.

Kristi studied with Taara for about a year, never knowing how long she would stay or what she should commit to. "Learning Kaumi was slow going," Kristi recalls, "but it was still a really good thing. I wouldn't change it even if I could because of the opportunity to build a relationship with Taara and her family."

LET'S DO THIS!

The in-between state did eventually come to an end and Kristi was able to take the long-awaited survey trip to the city of Iman, in the heartland of Kaumi society. She was surprised that, even with a head start in language, she couldn't do anything on her own. As a woman, she could only ride with certain taxi drivers who were known to be reliable, meaning she had to arrange her trips on the phone, which she found was beyond her limited language ability. People navigated by landmarks and area names that weren't on maps, so she also had to know where she wanted to go and communicate how to get there. "That scared me a little bit," Kristi admits. "I'm quite directionally challenged. It was a shock to realize, *Wow, it's going to be a big learning curve to figure out how to live here.*"

But mostly, Kristi was grateful to finally connect face-to-face with potential teammates. She says, "We had some really sweet times of prayer, and it was such a privilege to pray and worship God in that place after praying for the Kaumi for so long and imagining what it would be like to be in their homeland." Kristi ended the trip with the attitude, *Let's do this!* and officially joined the team working in Iman.

Then the implications sank in—*How am I going to tell everybody?* Many of her friends and supporters had hoped she would settle down in the U.S. and continue working with Kaumi refugees. Kristi was grateful for the experience gained with her temporary team but firmly believed Iman was the right place to lay the groundwork for a ministry career that might take her almost anywhere in the world.

NOW WHAT?

A few months after her survey trip, Kristi landed back in Iman with the expectation that she would live there for 18-24 months, although she was open to staying longer. She recognized the cue that she was entering a new world: As the plane landed, she donned the culturally mandated headscarf. For as long as she stayed in the country, she would need to cover her hair whenever she stepped outside her home, and that wasn't as easy as it sounds. Kaumi women seemed to keep their head scarves in place with an elusive combination of practice, friction and willpower. Kristi found herself worrying constantly about the scarf: *Is it slipping? How do I take my purse strap on and off my shoulder without bumping it? What if it falls off?*

For her first month in Iman, Kristi lived with a single teammate. Haley taught her practical tips, like keeping a headscarf by the door so she could grab it quickly if someone stopped by. Haley also arranged for two language teachers to come to the house on alternating days, and she introduced Kristi to other missionaries in the city. Kristi's first six months were set aside for adjustment and language learning. Then she would start working on a humanitarian project. Kristi visited the group's office and met some of the staff, but she was happy for the chance to focus on learning Kaumi and figuring out how to live in Iman.

In less than a month, Kristi's initial attitude of, *I can't believe I'm finally here!* morphed into, *What on earth am I doing here?* Her first moment of panic came when she woke up in the middle of the night to the sound of a flying cockroach trapped in a plastic bag. She gathered her courage and smashed it with her shoe, thinking, *This is ridiculous!*

But worse than cockroaches was the feeling of being stuck. Every morning, Kristi had a two- or three-hour language lesson at Haley's house. She tried to be a good hostess by serving tea and treats, and after class, she put on her sweater and scarf and walked her tutor to the gate. Then she would stand in the yard surrounded by concrete walls and wonder, *Now what?* Haley and her other teammates were working on development projects, but Kristi didn't yet have the language skills to contribute. She couldn't leave the house alone because she couldn't call a taxi driver and didn't have anywhere to go. As a woman, she couldn't wander the streets by herself and didn't have any friends to visit.

About three weeks in, the isolation and helplessness hit full force. *What did I think I could do here? I'm never going to be able to talk. I'm never going to be able to leave. I'm never going to be able to do anything.* Kristi couldn't even give up and go back to America because she couldn't get herself to the airport. Feeling stuck and helpless, she followed the common practice of generations of faithful missionaries in overwhelming situations: She cried about it. "I had a meltdown. And when I finished, I asked myself, *What* can *I do?*"

Kristi knew Haley sometimes sent the security guard out to buy street food, so she decided to try it. The guard spent his time in a little room by the front gate, and that day he happened to be napping. Kristi didn't know how to say, "I'm so sorry to disturb your nap, but would you please go buy me some lunch?" So, she just called out tentatively, "Hello?" until he roused himself. Then she said "beans, tomatoes," offered him a handful of cash and an empty bowl and waited to see what would happen.

The guard, who was familiar with the ways and limitations of foreigners, disappeared out the gate. In a few minutes, he returned and handed Kristi back the bowl, now full of black beans and diced tomatoes. It was exactly what she had hoped for—a single serving of lunch from a street vendor. That small victory pulled Kristi out of her slump, at least for the day.

A NEW NORMAL

A lot of Kristi's new life felt strange and uncomfortable at the beginning. For example, the humanitarian project manager occasionally sent security alerts to the staff. On any given day, Kristi might wake up to a text about a road closure or fighting outside the city. "I guess

I trusted my team a lot," Kristi explains. "I told them, 'I'm going to assume all this is normal unless you tell me differently.'"

Gradually the strangeness morphed into a sense of normalcy. Kristi started going on outings with other women. She found the central market loud and colorful and a welcome contrast after weeks of quiet, lonely afternoons at Haley's house. "You touch people the whole time and haggle for everything," Kristi remembers. A single missionary invited her over one evening to watch the pigeons, doves and kites from her roof. "We were above all the walls, and we could see the neighbors in their yards or coming home from shopping. For once I didn't feel enclosed. I just felt so privileged to pray for the Kaumi in their homeland. How many people get to do that?" Praying on that roof, Kristi finally thought, *I know why I'm here.*

After about a month in Iman, Kristi's team started talking about how things weren't quite normal. A rebel group was gradually taking control of villages in other parts of the country. Iman had been a very stable town. Chaos and violence simmered in other regions, but Iman itself always stayed relatively calm. Kristi adopted the mindset of her teammates: *This is a tense time, but it'll pass.* Besides, she was distracted by the opportunity to move into a house of her own. Two single women missionaries lived in separate houses with a shared yard, and Kristi had been invited to house-sit for one of them for a year. The property featured a giant tree with a trunk too wide to wrap her arms around and the shade and flowers provided a pleasant distraction from the cement walls. Kristi was thrilled with her new setup. *This is the beginning! I have my own place!* Haley's hospitality had been a gift, but she felt ready to start functioning more independently.

Kristi shared the compound not only with another missionary woman but also with a dog. He was a large, Rottweiler-esque creature who served as backup to the security guard. One of the first things Kristi heard about him was that he had recently bitten someone. Kristi wasn't a dog person, but she told herself, *I need to make friends with this dog. I have to be able to walk around the yard.* She didn't have enough language to befriend very many people yet, but she set about winning over the dog with food. One morning, he sauntered up to the porch where Kristi was sitting, casually sniffed her hand and then wandered off. "I was very proud of myself that we were friends," Kristi remembers.

The next morning, her time in Iman came to an abrupt end.

NO MORE NORMAL

Kristi's day started as usual with breakfast, quiet time and a language class. She prayed about the unrest brewing in other parts of the country but says she was "bopping along" thinking, *I live near a conflict zone. Things happen. My team will tell me if it's not fine anymore.* When the office manager announced a meeting for all the foreign staff that afternoon, her main concern was how to get there. *Oh no! I have to make it to the office all by myself!* But she managed it and joined about a dozen other foreign workers in a meeting room equipped with two couches and a few stray chairs. Someone had ordered lunch for the group, and Kristi fixed herself a plate of rice and chicken.

Once everyone assembled, the manager came straight to the point: "I'm sorry, guys. The powers that be decided we all have to leave." His phrasing stuck in Kristi's memory: *the powers that be.* The decision to evacuate had been made by the humanitarian group's leaders outside the country. Their main concern was the airport. While there had been no sustained fighting in the area, rebels had gradually taken control of the roads out of the city. If they advanced on the airport, the staff would be trapped. No matter how much humanitarian good they were doing, Westerners would not be looked on favorably by Muslim extremists. Iman was still technically peaceful, but it was a menacing peace. The "powers that be" gave their personnel two weeks to close out and evacuate. No one in Iman believed it was necessary.

Kristi describes the feeling in the room as "a very quiet swirl." A few people cried softly. Others seemed lost in thought. Some went straight to the details: *What do we do with our projects? What about our Kaumi co-workers? How do we say goodbye?* In a country known for unrest, everyone knew that evacuation could theoretically be necessary, but foreigners had never evacuated from Iman. They were in shock that it was happening now.

For Kristi, being in a room of strangers all processing a lot of emotion felt very uncomfortable. "I'd only been there a month. I wasn't attached to anyone in Iman yet. I wasn't in charge of anything. So, I didn't feel like I had anything to say." After a while, people started drifting away and she made her way home in a sort of daze.

While Kristi and her team worked for the humanitarian group in Iman, they also kept in close touch with Theresa, their Pioneers leader. On a Zoom call that night, Theresa helped them think through a basic plan. Frank and Eileen Goodman in Europe had extended a standing invitation to displaced workers from South Asia. The Iman team had designated their city on the Mediterranean as a "strategic waiting place" should it become necessary to evacuate.

Mission teams establish contingency plans in case they have to suddenly change locations for any number of reasons, but few expect to use them. Talking with Theresa, it suddenly became very real to the team: *We actually have to go to this strategic waiting place. How will we get there?* At the time, much of Europe still had COVID travel restrictions and quarantine requirements. Securing PCR tests in Iman that would be accepted at a European airport would not have been easy during a peaceful period, let alone when social and political upheaval was flaring up.

Kristi didn't realize how complicated getting out of Iman was until much later. Theresa took over the planning process. "You focus on getting ready to leave," she told the team, "and I'll work out the logistics." She researched airlines, COVID testing and quarantine requirements for a few days and then texted, "I'm going to meet you for a two-week debrief in Romania. I just booked your flights." Romania isn't an obvious stop-over point on the way from South Asia to Mediterranean Europe and neither Theresa nor anyone on the Iman team had ever been there. But Romania would allow them all to enter the country right away, and after two weeks they would be able to travel freely in Europe.

SLOW-MOTION EVACUATION

Kristi doesn't remember a lot of details from her final days in Iman. Two weeks is an awkward amount of time to close down your life. For the missionaries who had been in the country for years, it was not long enough. But two weeks was still a long time, especially for Kristi, who didn't have a household to pack up, friends to say goodbye to or a ministry to hand off. She moved back in with Haley because there was no point continuing to set up her own home.

Even though she continued language classes until a few days before the departure deadline, time dragged for Kristi. All the foreigners in Iman were grieving, but they weren't grieving the same things she was. Her losses were intangible—the ministry she had waited for and worked toward for more than two years, the relationships she longed to build with local women and the impact she hoped for through the humanitarian project she planned to join. Haley, on the other hand, was grieving the impending loss of people and places she had invested years in, at great personal risk and cost. And she had to pack, store or dispose of nearly all her physical possessions.

With virtually all of the foreigners in Iman leaving at once, Haley expected their homes would be looted. Kristi helped her choose one of her beautiful silk rugs and a few other souvenirs to keep and took pictures of all her piano music so she could replace it later. They gave a lot of things away and packed the rest neatly in the house. They knew it was wishful thinking to expect it would stay that way.

Haley and Kristi had some items too sensitive to risk falling into the hands of rebels or curious neighbors. Disposing of them is what Kristi describes as "the fun part of evacuating." Iman doesn't have the kind of trash system where you throw things away and no one ever sees them again. People sort through the trash by hand, looking for anything that can be reused. Kristi and her teammates also wanted to get rid of things that could not be easily burned. So, a few days before the departure deadline, they packed up a car and drove into the countryside. They found a dry, deserted well and took turns throwing things down it.

Kristi's computer had broken beyond repair during her brief time in Iman, but theoretically, someone might be able to recover sensitive information about her or about others and their work. So, she dropped it down the well. Her teammates threw in ministry materials, keys and books—anything they didn't want their neighbors or rebel fighters to find. There was a sense of relief and finality watching things disappear into the darkness. Each item took a full four seconds to hit bottom.

THE FAMILIAR UNKNOWN

Two weeks after the evacuation mandate was announced, Kristi and Haley drove to the airport with one suitcase each. Checkpoints had sprung up all over the city, many of them manned by armed men. But Haley and Kristi had no trouble getting through. Aside from the checkpoints, the city didn't feel different. Even the rebels were courteous, "Hi! How are you doing? Can we check out your car?" Everything seemed very normal except for the fact that nothing was normal.

For Kristi, leaving Iman felt like a return to the uncertainty of the past two years. *I don't know where I'm going. I don't know what's going to happen.* Unsettledness had become such a familiar feeling to her that it didn't seem strange anymore. More like, *Here we go again.*

Lands of Tea & Opportunity

Kristi Reid's Story
Part 2

WHO GOD STILL IS

Kristi thinks her departure from Iman would have been harder emotionally if her somewhat nebulous grief had not been dwarfed by the more obvious and concrete losses her teammates were facing. She says, "I felt like my role was to be there for my teammates, and I'm grateful for that. If I was left on my own, I think I really would have been depressed thinking about all my own problems, *Woe is me! I have to move again! I'm all by myself. Who's going to help me figure this out?*"

Theresa was there and ready to help. She had booked a hotel in a quaint town in the Carpathian Mountains. It was a weird way to visit Romania, but Kristi did get to tour a castle. Frank Goodman traveled up from the Mediterranean coast to co-lead the debrief with Theresa. Kristi had only met Frank briefly on a video call, but she had heard from other foreigners in Iman about the Goodmans' unheard-of planned departure. "They decided years in advance when they would leave," people marveled, "and then they left when they said they would. When does that happen?"

During their two-week debrief, the team worshipped together each day, and Kristi says it was stabilizing to pray for each other and the building tension around Iman. "We focused on God. Who He still is. And we prayed a lot for the people still in the country and for all the people who had to leave."

Kristi soon realized she had not yet processed a lot of the uncertainty and transitions of the past two years: deciding to move abroad, COVID delays, her time with the temporary team in the U.S., her arrival in Iman and now the sudden departure. During that whole time, she hadn't had one consistent person in her life. Her family couldn't fully understand what she had experienced overseas. Her teammates had only known her for a few months. No one had walked through the past decisions with her, and no one was going to live out her next decision with her, either.

Kristi knew she had a lot to sort through emotionally but found it very hard to talk about. Mostly, she just cried, which felt awkward because she didn't know either Theresa or Frank very well. "I was like, 'Sorry, guys! I can't answer your question. I'm just going to cry about it.' But it was really good to have the space to do that. I found out they are amazing people!"

KNOWNS AND UNKNOWNS

During the debrief, the team discussed how to move forward and whether they would continue to be a team. Each member had different priorities as they considered what to do next. Even if they hoped to return to Iman when the situation stabilized, they all realized it was likely to be a long wait. During their two weeks in

Romania, they decided to stay together for six months and help each other discern their next steps—steps which would likely take them in different directions.

Looking back, Kristi is surprised she was so set on continuing in overseas ministry. It would have been understandable to think, *I tried foreign missions, and it clearly hasn't worked. I'm going home.* Kristi thinks the reason she didn't feel a tug back to the U.S. is that it didn't feel like home. "I didn't fit in my hometown anymore. I never really settled on my temporary team, so returning there would feel like starting over. Going back to the U.S. didn't seem easier than any of the other options, honestly." Even as her emotions swirled in Romania, Kristi remained convinced, *I want to work with Kaumi people somewhere. I guess it's not going to be in their homeland.* She realized that as a newbie on the field and a beginning language student, she wouldn't be among the first missionaries to return to Iman, even when that became possible.

GRIEVING TOGETHER

The two weeks in Romania over, it was time to head to the "strategic waiting place," the Mediterranean city where the Goodmans lived. Kristi's first memory of Southern Europe is a wave of relief—*They let us in!* Part of her brain celebrated, *I'm in Europe! I should be excited!* Theresa insisted that the team do some sightseeing and enjoy the perks of their unsettled state. A different part of Kristi's brain ran a constant drumbeat: *What am I going to do? How long am I going to be here? Where do I go next?* The team settled at an Airbnb in what Kristi describes as "refugee central" downtown. Their apartment overlooked a large square that was a hangout for hundreds of South Asian immigrants, including many Kaumi families. Kristi got the sense that local people in that part of town were cautious, but for her, the presence of the Kaumi was comforting; they were the one consistent thread through the last two years. *This is great!* she thought, *I know how to dress and what to do.* At the same time, she enjoyed the freedom of not having to meet all the Kaumi cultural expectations. The refugees were also foreigners learning the ropes in a new place.

On her first night there, Kristi remembers looking out the window and seeing Frank and Eileen crossing the square to bring a hot dinner for the whole team. "They were very welcoming," she says, "and they made the transition so much easier." Haley had worked with the Goodmans years before when they still lived in Iman. Kristi considered any like-minded person who worked with the Kaumi to be an automatic friend.

A few days later, about three weeks after the team left South Asia, the building tension between the government, rebel forces and Islamic extremists erupted on a scale few people other than maybe "the powers that be" had anticipated. The city of Iman disintegrated into chaos. Armed fighters patrolled the streets and harassed civilians. Schools and businesses shut down, and hospitals scrambled to treat the wounded. Hundreds of Kaumi families fled in fear, clogging the airport and roads as they sought to escape the violence. Kristi's team and the Goodmans watched Kaumi-language news and social media posts with horror. The desperate scenes weren't just images on a screen—their friends' lives were in danger. They were shocked at the speed and brutality of the destruction.

The situation in Iman eventually grew so desperate that it attracted the attention of the international news media. When stories appeared in U.S. outlets, emails started pouring into Kristi's inbox from relieved friends and supporters. "Thank the Lord you're safe and out of the country!" many wrote. But Kristi wasn't thankful—she was grieving. In a theoretical sense, she was grateful that God had given foresight to the "powers that be" and spared her from the violence or a more chaotic evacuation, but her overwhelming emotion was loss. "My American friends' perspective felt very one-sided," she explains. "It's understandable because they knew me and cared about me, but it was hard to interact with people at the time. Think of all the people who were still in Iman!"

One thing Kristi did feel thankful for at the time was her relationship with the Goodmans. Frank and Eileen are not counselors, but they are, in Eileen's words, "Let's-eat-food-and-take-walks-and-talk kind of people." Kristi remembers, "They understood what was going on and talked things through with us. They kept us sane." And the feeling was mutual. Eileen wrote to friends in the U.S., "A sweet gift for us, personally, has been that our old team from Iman decided to evacuate here. Although the situation is grim, it is a blessing to have friends to grieve and process with on a level that we couldn't with others."

WAITING STRATEGICALLY

The displaced Iman team took the "strategic" in "strategic waiting place" to heart. Even as the situation in their former home disintegrated, they were looking for the next place they could serve Kaumi people who had been—or were about to be—displaced. They started by determining the major centers of the Kaumi diaspora, besides their anchor city on the Mediterranean coast. Mostly, they found them through word of mouth. The mission world runs on relationships. The refugee community is tied together through family connections. "Kaumi people have been fleeing South Asia for years," Kristi explains, "It's not a new thing."

It didn't take Kristi and her teammates long to get a general sense of where the Kaumi population centers were, and then they could do more specific research about those cities and the missionaries serving there. The team was based in the city for five months while they made survey trips to other locations. Kristi was glad to have teammates to compare notes and commiserate with and to once again be in a country where she could go to a park or coffee shop on her own to think and pray.

EXPLORING

The team started by exploring options in southern Europe. But while there was a lot to love about life and ministry on the Mediterranean, it didn't take long for Kristi to realize it wasn't a good fit for her at that point. Her first priority was still language learning, and while she did get some tutoring from a Kaumi refugee, she found it very hard to learn Kaumi in a context where so many people spoke English and other European languages. "I'm not an amazing language learner," she says, "I'm an average language learner, so I need significant immersion to really learn it."

Kristi started exploring options farther afield, returning to the Goodmans on the coast to rest and process in between. Those early visits helped crystallize her priorities: *I need to learn Kaumi or at least some form of Indo-Persian. And I'm too new on the field to start a ministry from scratch. I need to join someone I can learn from.*

With those parameters in mind, Kristi quickly narrowed her options. A predominantly Muslim Central Asian country kept rising to the top of her possibilities list, so she packed up again and headed out to explore. She found that a lot of missionaries had transitioned from South Asia to the country's capital, Lotfan, and that would provide some built-in community. The biggest draw was a language commonality. The national language shares a common Indo-Persian heritage with Kaumi. The basic grammatical structure was the same as Kaumi, and some vocabulary was the same. Kristi was pleased to find she could communicate, at least on a surface level, using the bits of Kaumi she had learned in the U.S., Iman and Europe.

The national government wanted to boost tourism and foreign investment, so Kristi anticipated that getting a visa would be relatively simple. The welcoming attitude toward foreigners, however, did not extend to Kaumi refugees. They were only allowed to live in a designated area just outside Lotfan. And there weren't as many Kaumi people as there were near the Goodmans or some of the other cities Kristi had researched. Based on the ratio of missionaries to refugees, the need was greater elsewhere. However, Lotfan provided the team structure Kristi had been looking for, with experienced missionaries focused on reaching the Kaumi. "Between that and the language overlap," Kristi explains, "it all clicked."

KEEPING ON GOING

After her trip to Lotfan, Kristi returned to the U.S. to spend Christmas with her family. As she began explaining her new plans to friends and supporters, she started to realize just how bizarre it all sounded. "The general feeling was confusion. Half of my conversations were just, 'Where have you been? What have you been doing? And why?'" The connecting thread between South Asia, Romania, southern Europe and Central Asia was not obvious. "I'm so thankful I could explain it in person," Kristi says, "rather than doing it from afar." She found some confirmation in repeating the story over and over. Her chain of decisions made sense with a little context, and her church affirmed her planned transition to Lotfan.

Kristi returned to the Mediterranean coast briefly and said goodbye to her Iman teammates before traveling on to Lotfan. The Goodmans weren't surprised that Kristi decided not to stay in their city. "I just respected her tenacity," Eileen says, "She spent years trying to get to the field, and then couldn't stay. She could have thrown it in and said, 'That's it, I'm done.' But she went on to Lotfan to learn from seasoned missionaries. She's a good example. If God calls you, keep on going. Don't let up."

DIVING IN DEEP

In the lead-up to her arrival in Central Asia, Kristi dreaded starting over. New city. New team. New culture. A new variation of a language. It was her fourth ministry location in 12 months. But once she arrived in Lotfan, a sort of euphoria kicked in. "I was so excited to have a place to be for a while that I found it pretty easy to reinvest."

The day after she landed in Central Asia, Kristi moved in with a local family for a four-month home stay. She was excited to learn a language by total immersion. While it wasn't a Kaumi family, she knew she had a lot to learn about how the majority people of Lotfan live daily life. She couldn't wait to jump in.

Kristi was hosted by a woman in her fifties who lived with her college-aged daughter, adult son, his wife and their two young children. The house itself was tiny, with a small cement yard and a pit toilet outside. Kristi's room was connected by interior windows to the kitchen on one side and the living room on the other, so she essentially lived in a fishbowl in the center of the house. Her windows had curtains, but the walls were very thin. "I felt like I knew everything that went on in the house, and they knew everything I was doing all the time too." Immersion was, after all, the purpose of the homestay.

For the first two weeks, Kristi never saw the adult son, Aizat. *Does he even live here?* she wondered. She soon learned that men typically spent their time outside the house, especially if the family had a female visitor. "They didn't know what to do with me because usually if a single woman was a guest in their house, Aizat wouldn't interact with her. With me it was confusing—*She lives in our house, so she's kind of part of the family, but she's still a guest and a single lady.*" After two weeks, the women in the family awkwardly introduced Kristi and Aizat. She didn't know what to say other than, "Hi! Nice to meet you. Thank you for letting me stay in your house." After that, the whole family treated her like another sister or cousin, and everything felt more normal.

One afternoon, Aizat came home from work unusually early and decided that they should all have a water fight. It was over 100 degrees outside that summer, and although the family had three air conditioning units, they never turned them on. They didn't use fans, either, so a water fight seemed like an excellent idea. Aizat ran around the house spraying a hose at the women through the windows, and they splashed him back with buckets from the inside. Kristi never expected to have so much fun in a conservative Muslim household. *What is going on?* she asked herself in shock, *This is not the image I had of them!*

But life was generally much more sedate than that. A lot of value in the homestay for Kristi was learning the mundane rhythms of life she would never see if she only visited local homes. She discovered, for example, that her host culture had a very different philosophy of sleep than she was used to. They had no concept of bedtime and did not value uninterrupted sleep. Instead, they dozed when they were tired. The kids roused the adults at will, and the lights in the kitchen came on whenever someone was hungry. Kristi soon realized she couldn't cope with their schedule. "For my sanity, we set the expectation, *Kristi locks her door at 10 or 11 at night and goes to bed, and she doesn't come out until 7 a.m.*" She learned to sleep wearing an eye mask and headphones.

One cultural stress point that never really went away was how to respond to the restrictions on Aizat's wife, Alena, as a young mom in a conservative family. She had to stay in the house with the curtains drawn unless she gained permission to go out from both her husband and her mother-in-law. Sometimes she complained to Kristi, "I want to go outside and play with the kids, but Aizat said no," or "I just want to go on a walk, but my mother-in-law said no." Alena's restrictions contrasted sharply with Kristi's freedom. It almost felt mean for Kristi to talk about her outings in front of Alena, knowing that she wished for the same opportunities.

But overall, Kristi learned a lot about navigating everyday life in a culturally appropriate way. For example, something as simple as refusing food felt very stressful at first. Her hosts always urged her, "Eat more! Eat more! Do you not like my food?" even though Kristi felt like she'd eaten enough for two people. By watching the family members interact, she learned it was completely acceptable to say, "Oh, thank you, I'll take some," and then not take anything. "They are my people now, and as long as I can verbalize my questions, they are the ones who help me figure things out."

And the learning wasn't all one-sided. Kristi's host family also got to observe her lifestyle, including her spiritual practices. "They know my teammates, but it's a different kind of knowing because I lived with them." The first time Kristi offered to pray for her host mom, "She didn't even know what to say because young people don't pray out loud here. That's not a thing, I came to find out." One of Kristi's favorite spiritual conversations came about because of a cultural blunder. Kristi forget that Muslims consider pigs unclean and showed Alena a cute photo of a litter of piglets born at her sister's farm. The significance didn't sink in until Alena asked, "Do you eat pork?"

Kristi answered honestly, "I do. What about you?"

"Oh no," Alena responded, "Our Holy Book says it's not allowed and it's dirty."

Kristi decided to make the most of the opportunity since she had already gone that far. "That's interesting. In my Holy Book, it says it's not what you eat that makes you clean or unclean, it's what's in your heart." Kristi was still an early language learner at that stage, and the conversation stretched the limits of her vocabulary and grammar. Alena listened, but Kristi wasn't sure she understood.

A few days later, as the family ate dinner around a tablecloth on the floor, Kristi suddenly realized Alena was describing their conversation: "Kristi eats pork because her Holy Book says our sins make us clean or unclean, not the food we eat." Kristi was amazed. "She was retelling the whole thing way better than I ever could." Alena told the story again a few days later to a group of guests. "My language wasn't great," Kristi acknowledges. "Yet I was able to share a short, little truth because of a photo I never would have shown Alena if I had thought about it. But what a great conversation to have! It opened the door later to more questions once the family realized that I do things differently for a reason. Most of them have never interacted with a believer."

COMING UP FOR AIR

While Kristi enjoyed her homestay experience, after four months she realized it was time to move out of the fishbowl and get a place of her own. Leaving was harder than she expected. "Because I so quickly jumped into deeply investing, it was hard on my heart." For the first few weeks, she struggled with guilt. "Alena couldn't do anything for herself. While I lived with her, I could be her advocate. Now I can't." At the same time, Kristi received frequent text messages from Alena and her mother-in-law, *Why haven't you come to visit us? You've been gone for so long! Do you not like my food? The kids cry when you're not here in the morning.* She remembers, "It didn't help in the transition when I was already in a fragile place emotionally." Kristi's team leaders helped her see that what sounded to her American ears like a guilt trip was the Central Asian way of saying, "I miss you." She learned to interpret the messages as something more along the lines of, *We love it when you visit. Please come back soon.*

VARIATIONS ON A THEME

Ever since joining her temporary team in the U.S., Kristi had been trying to learn the Kaumi language. The challenge in Lotfan was that the majority of the population spoke an Indo-Persian dialect, but it wasn't exactly Kaumi. Kristi didn't have to learn a separate language for everyday interactions with locals like her homestay family, but she had to learn variations on a theme. She explains, "There are literary words that align more closely with Kaumi, and then there are street words that people use every day, and there are loan words from other nearby languages. If I just learn the street language, I won't understand or be understood by Kaumi speakers very well. Sometimes I have to learn four words for one thing so that I can communicate with everyone."

Even as Kristi settled into a more normal rhythm of life in Lotfan, questions lingered about what exactly she was doing there. Her goal had always been to work with Kaumi refugees, but she didn't interact with any during her homestay. She began to wonder, *God, are You going to take Kaumi people out of the picture? Am I doing the right thing?*

God answered her questions in part through another foreign student at Kristi's language school who had also worked in Iman. Soon after Kristi moved out of her homestay, this friend pulled her aside. "I've been asked to teach English in the Kaumi refugee settlement," she said. "I'd feel more confident doing it with someone else. Do you want to join me?"

Kristi jumped at the chance and started teaching English a few hours a week to Kaumi women. "The opportunity came in the perfect timing," she says. "I wasn't in my homestay anymore, so I was more in control of my time and I didn't have to go home to a cross-cultural situation every night. Why was I so worried about ministry opportunities? God had it covered the whole time."

Kristi found that even just six weeks in Iman gave her a measure of common ground with the Kaumi women who came to her English classes. "I know some of the places they talk about. I keep up with the news. I'm learning Kaumi words, not just the local street language, and I dress like them. I think they realize, *Oh, she does understand some things,* and they're more ready to open their hearts a little bit and let me in."

JUST AS FAITHFUL, LESS SURE

Even before going to the field, Kristi had heard enough stories to know that missionaries didn't always stay forever. But that still seemed like the goal. *You go and you stay. That means you're being faithful. That means you heard God right.* Over the last few years, Kristi has developed a richer and less rigid understanding of faithfulness. She has no idea how long she'll be in Lotfan. She hopes to have another 12-18 months. But she thought the same thing about Iman. Undoubtedly, God has more surprises ahead for her. "All I can do is be faithful where I am," she says, "and bring lots of people in to help me discern when it's time to take another step. I'm quicker to ask people to discern with me now than I used to be because I'm not quite as sure what it means to be faithful right this moment. And that's a good thing."

Ministry to Kaumi women took Kristi to four countries in her first 12 months on the field. And yet, in some ways, not that much has changed since she stood in Jamila's living room, trying to explain the gospel in simple words with seven kids under 10 bouncing off the walls. Life is still chaotic. Language is still a challenge. Ministry still involves copious amounts of tea. And every once in a while, Kristi is still amazed to realize, *God coordinated this moment and gave me something to share.* And she's relieved, too, to remember that Jamila couldn't always keep her headscarf on either.

Available, Brave & Crazy

David & Ashley Moore's Story
Part 1

COMPLETELY AVAILABLE

David Moore grew up listening to his dad's vinyl records—Simon and Garfunkel, the Beatles and Petra, a big-hair 80s Christian band. He remembers lying on the floor next to the record player doing his homework and crying with conviction as Petra's *This Means War* album pledged:

I am available. I am available.
I will go when You say go.
I am available. I am available.
I will stop when You say no.
My whole life was incomplete
Until I laid it at Your feet.
So use me as You will.
I am available.

"I'll go wherever you ask me to," David promised the Lord, which meant he'd do what missionaries in biographies did—move to the ends of the earth, endure trials and see multitudes saved.

A LITTLE SKEPTICAL

Ashley's journey into missions started when she met David during their first year of college. He told her right off the bat, "I've wanted to be a missionary since I was 12." Ashley wasn't convinced. Most people don't follow through on their middle school career aspirations. But she liked David, and they started dating. During their sophomore year, they studied abroad together for a semester in Guatemala. By that point, Ashley had warmed up to the idea of missions enough to switch her major to Spanish and ESL. She saw teaching English as the perfect missionary job but still wasn't sure if she was cut out for cross-cultural ministry.

In their junior year, David and Ashley attended a missions conference emphasizing the needs of the unreached, specifically the Muslim world. David told Ashley afterward, "I feel like the Lord told me I'm supposed to go to Southeast Asia." All Ashley knew about that part of the world was that it had lots of islands, but David explained his logic. Of all the Muslim nations, those in Southeast Asia most closely resembled the Hispanic cultures they both loved, with a lush, tropical climate and warm, outgoing people.

David must have explained his mindset shift in a very charming way because Ashley did not second-guess their relationship. Instead, she spent Christmas break asking the Lord what He might have for her. Since middle school, David had been making deliberate choices to prepare himself for cross-cultural missions. Ashley had not. But that Christmas season, the Lord opened her eyes to the ways He had been preparing her anyway.

Although she was young, Ashley had ministry experience as a

camp counselor and high school worship team leader and had been on several mission trips. She had also developed a love of travel through international choir tours and studying abroad. Ashley's wanderlust stands in stark contrast to the rest of her family, who much prefer the familiarity and comfort of home to the unknowns and inconveniences of faraway adventures. She felt the Lord showing her, *Look at all these things I did in your life, not David's. Look at the mission trips I sent you on and how much you loved learning a language. I've been preparing you for overseas ministry even though you didn't realize it.*

EXPLORING

By May of their junior year, David was still more confident in his call to be a missionary than in his call to marry Ashley. He wondered, *Would it be loving to ask her to follow me into the unknown of Muslim Southeast Asia?* David now looks back on his perspective as somewhat self-righteous, but at the time, being totally available to the Lord included a willingness to be single.

The only way David saw to settle the issue was to visit Southeast Asia. With summer break only a few weeks away, he hurriedly emailed every missionary he knew. A family his parents supported introduced David to Robert and Michelle, Pioneers team leaders who agreed to host him for a three-week visit. David knew nothing of the city or surrounding people groups, but he took the opportunity, praying as he went, *Lord, can we bring you more glory here as a couple, or is this not a fit for Ashley?*

Ashley, by that point, was ready to say yes to both a ring and long-term missions, although she knew it would be the hardest thing she had ever done. She didn't have to wait long for David to decide. Although he didn't formally propose until the following February, from the tone of his letters during the trip, Ashley knew her future would include a round-the-world adventure.

CONFIRMING

David's main hesitation about marrying Ashley was that she did not have a specific call to be a missionary in Southeast Asia. She told him, "I see how God has worked in my life to equip me to answer the Great Commission among an unreached people group. But I don't feel a call to a specific place." David was skeptical of that heart posture. It was not the type of missionary call he had read about and not what he envisioned lying on the floor listening to Petra albums. God was supposed to tell each missionary exactly where to go.

On his first few nights in Southeast Asia, David stayed up late talking with Robert and Michelle about their decision to move to the field. To his shock, he discovered that Michelle didn't have a people group-specific calling, either. She would have happily followed Robert anywhere in the world. As David processed her story and heard how the Lord had used her in ministry, he knew God had answered his main prayer. He felt the freedom to serve together with Ashley, bringing both of their giftings to the ministry.

PREPARING

David and Ashley married in December 2006, and both started teaching in public schools. For the next five years, they focused on preparing for the field. The new Mr. and Mrs. Moore did not wait to cross the ocean before connecting with Muslims. They volunteered with a ministry in their city that reached out to immigrant families through tutoring programs. Most of their students were from a culture in East Africa, and the Moores grew to appreciate the East

African culture and idiosyncrasies and the people's strength of character, deeply entwined with their Muslim faith.

While David and Ashley enjoyed their stateside tutoring ministry, their eyes were firmly fixed on Southeast Asia. They planned to pay off their student loans and have their first baby at home, then head overseas. Ashley was pregnant with Sophia when they joined Pioneers in December 2011. Theoretically, David and Ashley went to the orientation program open-minded about where they would serve, but Ashley says they only pretended to be open-minded. Their commitment to joining Robert and Michelle's team never wavered.

Once they officially joined the mission agency, a trip to visit Robert and Michelle confirmed a fit for both David and Ashley. A highlight was teaching English at an after-school program the team had started in a poorer neighborhood. At the end of an afternoon teaching action verbs to the children, they realized, *We're specifically equipped to serve here. We're good at this!*

Church planting is an inherently long-term task, and David and Ashley's team set an example of faithfulness. Robert and Michelle had been on the field for almost 20 years and all the other team members had at least 10 years of experience. The Moores saw them as mentors to learn from and emulate. David promised himself, *I'm not going to be one of those missionaries who quits.* Ashley shared David's long-term outlook. She pictured having more children and raising them in Southeast Asia. She was already processing schooling options for one-year-old Sophia. The Moores were going to be one of those missionary families who went to the field, loved it and stayed forever. At least, they were available to be one of those families.

LAUNCHING OUT

Ashley was correct in her prediction that moving to Southeast Asia would be hard. She and David faced all the common challenges of starting life over in a new world: language learning, culture shock and the need to build new relationship networks. During their first rainy season, a roof leak migrated through their house from room to room, dripping from corners and light fixtures and occasionally reducing Ashley to a puddle on the floor, crying, "I just want to go back to America where our house never leaked." Sophia was a toddler and the Moores soon welcomed a new baby, Aiden. "Having a C-section overseas is no joke," Ashley remembers. "It felt brave and crazy."

For David, the transition was more rational than emotional. "In some ways," he explains, "I decided it was home before we moved there." They both made steady progress in language and culture acquisition and mostly enjoyed the process. Gradually, their lives settled into a rhythm. Life on their team, however, was much different than they anticipated.

RECALIBRATING

David and Ashley had an eight-year relationship with Robert and Michelle before arriving on the field. However, about a year before the Moores moved to Southeast Asia, Robert and Michelle accepted a new role as area leaders overseeing several teams. They broke the news to the Moores, "We're not going to be your team leaders after all." Less than six months after David and Ashley arrived in Southeast Asia, the new team leaders who replaced Robert and Michelle announced that they were also stepping down and moving to another city. That meant the team now consisted of David and Ashley, a newly arrived single woman who soon moved away and a newlywed couple. Eighteen months after joining what they considered "the most stable missionary team in the world," David and Ashley were tapped to lead what felt like an entirely different team.

As the Moores finished full-time language study and switched their focus to full-time ministry, they realized that their team of four adults—two of whom were moms of preschoolers—had limited capacity. They didn't have the ability or vision to continue the after-school program their team had invested in for over a decade. So, David and Ashley closed down the project that had first attracted them to the team. "There was a heaviness," they remember, "of being responsible for ending something that had been a big part of our identity coming into the work."

The second major ministry adjustment was shifting focus from training lots of people in disciple-making skills to focusing on a few. During the Moores' first two years on the field, their team had helped to train about a thousand local believers in church planting principles. But after two years, they could only identify one trainee who was putting theory into practice. They needed a new strategy, so they asked the Lord, *What are Your plans? How can we follow You in that direction?* The team soon identified three couples among their local believing friends who had a vision for self-reproducing house churches among their focus people group. The team committed to investing more than half their time and energy to support and encourage those three couples.

In two years, David and Ashley had moved around the world, learned a new language and culture and substantially re-shaped a team that had developed for decades under the guiding hand of people they deeply respected. The responsibility felt heavy. Yet the freedom was energizing.

Focusing on building trust in a smaller group of relationships came more naturally to David and Ashley than large trainings.

Tuesdays soon became the highlight of their week. One of the three core partners came to the Moores' house at about 3 p.m. They prayed together and reviewed key Scripture passages, and then the two men went to public places to search for spiritually open people. They would visit roadside stands or a university campus or walk through neighborhoods intentionally starting spiritual conversations. They returned home at 10 or 11 p.m. and prayed for the people who had shown interest.

On a few occasions, the Tuesday outings were marred by what David considered spiritual warfare. His fingers would start to tingle and then go numb one by one. Or he would see a black blob over the words in the center of his vision as he read Scripture. Medical friends suggested he was having migraines.

One Tuesday evening, David and his local partner met an elderly man with a history of sorcery, black magic and violence. Their simple conversation developed into a year-long Bible study from Genesis through the Gospels. The old man began to confess his faith in Jesus in his prayers: "I know You are the Son of God. I know You can forgive my sins. I know You died and rose again." Watching his transformation crystallized David and Ashley's ministry vision. They looked forward to investing many years in that type of relationship.

After an intense first three years on the field, David and Ashley were set to take a seven-month home assignment in 2016. They planned to visit supporters, introduce their family to Aiden, give birth to their third child and return to Southeast Asia just after Christmas. Leaving for the States was surprisingly hard. After three years of regularly thinking, *I can't wait to go home,* Ashley now found herself crying over the idea of leaving Southeast Asia. They had established a life and ministry they enjoyed, despite the challenges. They had deep friendships and a home that felt like a sanctuary, despite the leaks. "I want to go home," Ashley told David, "But I don't want to go home because this is home." They boarded their first flight to the U.S. with a sense of urgency to return to the field when the time came.

"LET'S TAKE A WALK"

David and Ashley and their kids landed back in the U.S. with people to see, stories to tell and a case of the flu. They bounced between friends' houses and enjoyed reconnecting with family and church partners they hadn't seen in three years. From May to September, they stayed in 13 homes.

Soon after the Moores landed in the U.S., David's mom started pestering him to see a neurologist about his occasional vision loss and numbness. To allay what he considered to be her hyper-vigilance, he agreed. The Moores were so confident it was just migraines that Ashley—10 days away from a scheduled C-section—didn't go to the appointment. The neurologist was 99% sure David was right about the migraines but ordered an MRI to rule out the 1% possibility of something else. He ordered a high-contrast MRI. When that was done, he knocked on the door of the changing room and said, "Come on, let's take a walk."

Staring at the MRI results in the neurologist's office, David thought, *That glowing white blob on one side of my brain doesn't seem like something that's on a normal person's brain.* The neurologist assured him, "If you're going to have a brain tumor, you've won the lottery with this one. It's in the perfect spot and it's slow growing. We should be able to take it out without causing any cognitive deficit."

David went outside and lay down in a patch of grass near the doctor's office. He remembers it was a beautiful day. He was shivering from the shock of the news and gratefully soaked in the calming sunshine as he talked to the Lord about what had just happened. He didn't want to tell Ashley the diagnosis over the phone and had a string of meetings that afternoon and evening which it didn't occur to him to cancel. It wasn't until 10 p.m. that David finally sat Ashley down, told her he had a brain tumor and then held her while she cried.

IMPLICATIONS

While the diagnosis was a shock, David soon came to see it as just one more obstacle to overcome. In his own words, "My mindset in encountering obstacles was that you beat them. That's one of the trademarks that define people of character." He admits that some of that attitude stemmed from pride. "I thought of myself as an impressive person. And I was competitive. I lived for obstacles." When the doctor estimated it would take a year to recover from surgery, David mentally cut that in half. From his perspective, a brain tumor was inconvenient but didn't have to interrupt their plans. They would still go back to Southeast Asia in January as planned.

Ashley, however, felt utterly overwhelmed. She remembers crying in bed, *How on earth am I going to parent three children by myself?* And she was angry at God. *I just finally decided Southeast Asia is home, and now this is happening. Why did You even bring us there?* In her grief and confusion, she wondered, *Haven't we already gone through enough hard things?*

Looking back, Ashley can see one clear reason the Lord took them to Asia: She doesn't think she could have weathered the coming storm if she hadn't first moved overseas. She learned so much more about perseverance and how to lean on God in those three years abroad than she ever did in the U.S. Still, she wasn't entirely happy about it, confiding in David, "God was sure sneaky if He only brought us there to make me strong enough to deal with this." Nevertheless, Ashley still clung to Him, writing in her journal, *Jesus, redeem this terrible time. May I be safe in Your arms, even as it feels like every-thing is falling apart.*

To complicate matters, David and Ashley were processing the terrible news during the last few days of Ashley's pregnancy. Ava was born 10 days after David's initial diagnosis. By God's grace, she was a calm baby. "The Lord knew I needed that," Ashley says.

The Moores scheduled David's surgery exactly eight weeks after Ava's birth so Ashley would be fully recovered from the C-section and able to lift and care for the kids. The oncologists and surgeons David consulted all agreed with the neurologist's initial conclusions: His tumor was optimally placed for surgery. He could anticipate a full recovery with no deficits. The positive prognosis fed into David's narrative. He knew this was the kind of setback that would prevent some people from continuing on the mission field, but he would lead his family and persevere through it, glorifying God—and probably impressing a lot of people—along the way.

Available, Brave & Crazy

David & Ashley Moore's Story
Part 2

AFTERMATH

David woke up from surgery in October of 2016 to find two of every-thing, six feet apart, in his hospital room. His severe double vision came as a complete surprise because the surgery had gone perfectly. David's doctors did not know why it happened but predicted his vision would improve rapidly in the next few weeks and then plateau. But week after week, he saw almost no improvement. His brain soon learned how to navigate a distorted view of the world, but it took a huge amount of energy. Simple tasks felt overwhelming.

In January, when David and Ashley had hoped to be on their way back to Southeast Asia, David was still sleeping 16 hours a day and struggling to function. He was told his vision would not improve anymore and paid $700 for a pair of glasses with such an extreme correction that the prescription baffled his local optom-etrist. However, at a follow-up appointment just a few weeks later, the ophthalmologist was dumbfounded to discover that David's eyes had improved rapidly way outside the normal time frame. "This never happens," he told David. "Do you want to wear glasses? You don't actually need to." The unexpected healing of David's eyes felt like a special reassurance from God, *I know this has been hard, but I'm still with you.*

DOING HARD THINGS

Once it became clear that the Moores' return to the field would be delayed, they tried to make the most of the extra time in the U.S. David signed up for an online ESL certification class which would make it easier for him to get a long-term visa in Southeast Asia. The class included an in-person student teaching experience. Even though he was only a few months post-op, David wasn't worried. He had already taught school for six years and remembers thinking, *I hope I don't make the other people in the class feel insecure.*

David needn't have worried. The teaching intensive consisted of eight lessons. After every class, David met with his instructor to go over what he needed to do the next day to pass. He spent nine hours preparing for each lesson and failed every one of them. He simply couldn't process and communicate the material. Walking back from the last class in a daze, David texted his brother, "I used to be able to do hard things." In his mind, returning to the mission field hinged on passing the ESL course, and despite the brain tumor and double vision, David was still certain they were supposed to go back. But after failing the course, he wasn't sure if he was capable of it. His world crumbled as he realized, *I can't do hard things anymore.*

David was shocked to discover he wasn't functioning normally. Ashley was not. Ever since the surgery, she had been telling David he was different. "You're so insensitive," she insisted, "You're not showing any empathy at all." David responded with anger. He had always been analytical and rational rather than sensitive and emotional. That was nothing new. He couldn't cope with Ashley's grief and what felt like unfair accusations.

David found overstimulating situations particularly challenging. If the kids acted up and got loud at the dinner table, he became overwhelmed. If Ashley didn't intervene, he grew frustrated. David's irritability caused Ashley to avoid leaving him alone with the kids. She didn't trust him to respond lovingly if they misbehaved, which made him even angrier. "We couldn't wade those waters by ourselves," David and Ashley realized, so they started intensive marriage counseling.

After the student teaching disaster, David had to accept that his brain surgery had left him with a significant cognitive deficit. As devastating as that realization was, it at least opened the door for him to communicate more openly with Ashley. David returned home from the ESL class and told her, "You're right. I'm not the same person anymore."

NO MAN'S LAND

Ever since David's diagnosis, the Moores had kept in close contact with their sending church pastor and Blake, their point person at Pioneers. Both of them would be part of discerning when David and Ashley were ready to return to the field. David was frustrated that Blake kept adding an "if" to that question. He encouraged the Moores to work on a backup plan. To David, the only way back to Southeast Asia was through single-minded focus and determination. There was no room for uncertainty and no need for a backup plan.

In March of 2017, David and Ashley joined a week-long debriefing conference at the agency's office in Orlando. During one of the breaks,

David went for a jog. The lyrics running through his head were from the Petra song that had crystallized his missionary zeal years before:

I am available. I am available.

I will go when You say go.

I am available. I am available.

The next line hit him with the force of a physical impact:

I will stop when You say no.

In David's words, "At that moment, I knew that God was taking Southeast Asia away." Was he available, even for that?

Later that day, David shared with Blake and a small group at the conference how that line had hit him "I feel like I have a bunch of symptoms of depression. We can't go back on the field if I'm struggling with mental health." They pushed back on the finality of that conclusion, encouraging David to give himself more time to heal before deciding.

TESTING THE WATERS

By the summer of 2017, things had stabilized somewhat for David and Ashley. Counseling had given them coping mechanisms and the conflict in their marriage had gradually reduced. They decided to take a short trip back to Southeast Asia to see how they managed in a cross-cultural situation. The Moores' entire time in the U.S. had been stressful and discombobulated. They didn't have a steady home, job or routine. But they knew how to live in Southeast Asia. Going back, even temporarily, felt like returning to normalcy.

For the first few days, the Moores enjoyed reconnecting with teammates and local friends. David was determined to make the most of the trip. *I'm going to get myself together for two weeks so we can come back in the fall.* Then they traveled to an area conference in another city, and things fell apart. David still struggled in overstimulating environments, and Southeast Asia is the land of overstimulation. On the first morning of the conference, David and Ashley fell into one of their conflict cycles. "That first morning," David remembers, "We knew we couldn't come back in the near future." Ashley agrees, "It was harder than we thought."

SINKING IN

Over the next school year, David worked as a substitute teacher to build his mental stamina. By the middle of 2018, he was working full days and it was time to make a decision about returning to the field. For two years, David and Ashley had been moving their departure back in three-to-six-month increments. Sophia's most common bedtime prayer was still, "God, help us go back to Asia as soon as possible." They couldn't keep living with one foot on each side of the ocean, and they couldn't stay on medical leave indefinitely.

Over a Zoom call, Blake and the Moores' sending church pastor told David and Ashley that they were not in support of them going back to Southeast Asia for the foreseeable future. David and Ashley gradually came to own that decision and receive it as godly wisdom. While it hurt, they believed that closing the door on a return to the field put them in a healthier position than the continual uncertainty and tension they had been living in. They asked themselves, *Could God actually care more about molding us to become more like His Son than He cares about our overseas ministry?* And more practically, *Are the challenges in our marriage directly related to the chunk of David's brain that was removed?* The answer to both questions seemed to be yes.

For David, the hardest part about the news was having to tell Sophia. He had hoped to fulfill her wish to return to Southeast Asia. Ashley felt grief mixed with relief. She wanted to go back to the field, but it also seemed overwhelming. In some ways, much of her life would be the same no matter where they lived. With three preschoolers, she didn't have a lot of capacity for ministry outside her home. That made it easier to let go of Southeast Asia.

But after the relief came the panic. *How are we going to survive? How will we get benefits?* Ashley is a planner, and they had no plan. The middle of August is a bad time to start looking for a full-time teaching job. David didn't get health insurance as a substitute, so Ashley started researching companies that gave benefits to part-time workers. *I don't know what to do right now,* she thought, *There's too many things.*

David doesn't remember a sense of panic after Pioneers and their church decided they should stay in the U.S. indefinitely. He maintained the same determination as always, just redirected his focus from getting back to Southeast Asia to overcoming the obstacles of staying in the U.S., like a job, insurance and a place to live. But he acknowledges, "I might be looking back with rose-colored glasses."

REENGAGING

To both David and Ashley's relief, the uncertainty didn't last long. A few months before it was decided that the Moores would remain in the U.S., David's childhood missions pastor had told them, "I don't know where the Lord will lead you guys, but if you need a job here, let me know." It turned out that he was now overseeing the tutoring ministry the Moores had volunteered with before going to Southeast Asia. When David called to say he needed a job, the leadership team had just closed the interviews for a full-time program director. They told David they'd consider him if he could come in that afternoon. At the end of the interview, they said, "We already knew you were the person we wanted as long as you and Ashley are both in agreement."

While the Moores had resisted the idea of developing a backup plan in case they had to remain in the States, the Lord had been laying the foundation for their next chapter of ministry for almost a decade. After three years of uncertainty and waiting, they confirmed a new ministry role within 10 days of their decision to stay in the U.S. They also joined a team reaching out to immigrants in their city which they hadn't realized existed. The certainty was a relief, but more importantly, it was stimulating to have a mission again. The Lord hadn't responded as they had hoped to their prayers to return to Southeast Asia, but David and Ashley felt Him assuring them, *I still have you by My right hand. I'm still here.*

CLOSURE

The transition hasn't been entirely seamless. David and Ashley still have suitcases in storage in Southeast Asia, although the volume dwindles as things disintegrate in the tropical heat and humidity. When they visited in 2017, the rental contract on their house was about to expire, so they gave a lot of their stuff away, saving some in the hopes of returning. At the time, the door back to Southeast Asia wasn't closed. There was always a crack. But David and Ashley now consider themselves to be in the U.S. for the long haul. "In one sense," they admit, "if the Lord called us there before, what's to say He wouldn't again? But it seems unlikely."

One of the hardest things about not returning was the feeling that they were letting down their national partners. They didn't want to be those people who said they were coming back and then didn't. Granted, they had a very valid reason, but it still somehow felt like a betrayal. Once the decision was made, David texted Arif, a gifted evangelist and strategist who had the vision to see self-sustaining churches in every village in their region. Being a partner and friend to Arif was one of David's strongest motivations for returning to the field. When he explained he wouldn't be able to do that, Arif responded, "Honestly, most Western missionaries stay here too long. I wish more people were in your shoes."

That's not the typical response of national believers when their Western partners leave the field. It wasn't even a polite Christianese response—*It's okay, I'll pray for you.* It was a unique release—*Yeah, it's probably better that you don't come back*—so in character with Arif's passion for ministry that David says it didn't even sting. "It gave us a lot of peace, feeling like the work was moving on without us. They didn't need me. The Lord was still working despite our departure." And He continued to work. Over the next 18 months, the Moores' ministry partners in Southeast Asia reported a wave of baptisms and multiplying house churches. David and Ashley celebrate the lasting fruit the Lord is producing and the chance they had to play a part—even temporarily—in the harvest.

While the Lord was gracious to provide closure and comfort for David and Ashley, they still find it hard to tell the story. "When people haven't had the experience of really trying to immerse themselves in another culture incarnationally, it's hard to express the gravity of changing your focus to another culture," David explains. The Moores have been blessed with a core group of friends and supporters who get it. "They understand how deep the commitment was and how immersive the process was in connecting with Southeast Asia. And how momentum started there, and the pain when we stopped being able to participate in it."

IMPACT

While in some ways David and Ashley are stepping back into a familiar tutoring ministry after almost 10 years away, they've learned and changed a lot in the meantime. David's experience working shoulder-to-shoulder with local believers in Southeast Asia and focusing on multiplying disciples has forever changed his approach to ministry. When he interacts with the East Africans he once again serves, he sees himself as a co-worker and a learner, not a Western expert with all the answers. He encourages his believing volunteers to adopt a similar posture with students who express openness to spiritual conversations. David coaches them on how to introduce Muslim friends to Scripture in ways that resonate with their culture and worldview.

David has also started a program for tutors to learn one of the East African languages. In Southeast Asia, he experienced how language-learning fosters close relationships. By taking on the role of students, David and other tutors demonstrate humility. "You're becoming like a baby. You're making yourself super vulnerable. They're seeing you struggle through things and persevere and depend on God."

For Ashley, her experience overseas impacts her relationships with people who are crossing cultural barriers. Last year, she tutored a first grader and grew close with his mother. Even though Ashley has never been to the family's home country in East Africa, the mom seemed more comfortable and open once she knew that Ashley has also lived internationally with children. The family later decided to leave the U.S. and move to North Africa, another major cultural adjustment. The mother flooded Ashley with questions: *How do you know what to pack? Where do you buy a power adapter?* And once they landed in their new home, her first text to Ashley read, *The language barrier is hard. I know you know what that feels like.*

STILL AVAILABLE

Ashley remembers going to the field with the expectation that it would be hard for a while, and they would have to persevere, then they would fall in love with their host country and live there until they were old and gray. Cross-cultural life would get easier over time. After these last few years of struggle in both ministry and marriage, she now realizes, "There is a lot of waking up every day and choosing to be faithful even if it might not get easier tomorrow. I had never considered that it would be this hard a lot of the time."

Through their years of marriage counseling, David came to see that his primary area of sin is self-righteousness. "I always said I was willing to die to myself by going to the mission field. I'm willing to get on a plane and move somewhere I can do impressive things. But am I willing to stay here and let Jesus put my self-righteousness to death? Am I willing to make disciples and walk in the Great Commission from a place of dependency and weakness?"

David and Ashley still embrace and live out the theme of the Petra song. They are still available to the Lord and are still committed to making disciples of all the peoples of the world. But David has a different perspective now when it comes to his part in that global mission. He has come to accept, and even find comfort in the fact that, as he puts it, "God gets to choose how He uses me to bring Himself the most glory."

Of War & Wallpaper

James & Lisa Walker's Story
Part 1

YES, NO OR OTHERWISE

After her first date with James, people warned Lisa she was making a mistake. Her friends and even one of her professors chided her, "Why are you dating a youth pastor? You're a missions major!"

They had a point. The next time Lisa saw James, instead of greeting him with a hello, she launched straight to the heart of the issue: "Are you interested in missions or not?"

James didn't consider that a yes-or-no question. "I'm willing to go wherever God wants me to serve," he told her. That answer earned him a second date, and then another, as they explored what ministry together might look like. A year later, in 1992, James and Lisa became Mr. and Mrs. Walker.

James describes ministry decision-making as the convergence of three elements: where you go, what you do and who you do it with. "For some people," he explains, "the place solidifies first, and they're certain, *I'm going to be a missionary in this particular country.* For other people, the type of ministry lines up first. For us, it was our relationship. We knew God wanted us together. The rest was just real estate."

NEW REAL ESTATE

After two years of marriage and youth ministry, the Walkers felt the Lord drawing them to a new ministry farther from home. They joined Pioneers in 1994 and committed to a team in the city of Moigorod in the just-barely-former Soviet Union.

Moigorod wasn't an obvious location to begin a missionary career. During the Cold War, it had manufactured nuclear warheads and had therefore been treated as something of a state secret. When the Walkers arrived, the city's location still wasn't identified on most maps—even though it had a population of well over half a million, about the same as present-day Memphis or Detroit. To make matters worse, as James and Lisa prepared for the move, the team they intended to join disintegrated. Within about six months everyone left except for a single woman whose visa situation appeared quite tenuous. *Wow,* Lisa thought, *This team isn't even going to be there by the time we move. Lord, really?*

The Walkers still had reasons to stay the course. James loved teaching, discipleship and working with youth. Lisa had done a short-term trip to Turkey in college and wanted to serve Muslims. Moigorod brought it all together. The team had established a training institute offering computer and English classes for young adults. The programs allowed them to build relationships with Turkic Muslims living as a minority group in a post-Soviet context. James and Lisa were excited about teaching at the institute, befriending young people and hosting short-term teams from the U.S. They also hoped to encourage the Slavic churches of Moigorod to reach out to their Muslim neighbors. As a practical consideration, James suffered from asthma and that limited their location options to places with relatively clean air. A visit to Moigorod confirmed the air quality would work for him.

James and Lisa weren't put off by the dispersion of their intended team. When they visited, they connected well with the national staff at the training institute and other local believers. Rebuilding the team would take time, but the Walkers had time. As Lisa explains, "I wanted to be long-term. We saw ourselves as 'lifers.'" But even she admits, "What we meant by 'lifers' wasn't completely defined."

LIFERS

Lisa Walker remained fully committed to a long-term vision for ministry as they sold off their belongings in the U.S., said goodbye to family and friends and boarded each flight toward their new home. She was excited to be a "lifer" as they rocked along for hours on the Soviet-era train from the capital to Moigorod. She was all in up until the moment she and James walked through the door of their new apartment for the first time. And then she regretted everything.

"It was so ugly," Lisa remembers. Garish purple and orange wallpaper draped the front hallway, and the rest of the apartment wasn't any better. "I just remember looking around and thinking, *How can I make this home?*"

When Lisa crawled into the lumpy bed that first night, she told James, "We made a big mistake. Can we please just go home?"

He assured her, "We can go home tomorrow."

"It was just shocking," Lisa explains. She had visited Moigorod before, but it felt so different to be there permanently. "It felt so foreign. And uncomfortable. It wasn't that I wasn't up for adventure, and I didn't need luxury. But the enormity of what we had done hit all at once. *I just moved to a different continent. I don't know anyone. I don't know the language.* I felt so incredibly vulnerable."

The next night, Lisa repeated her plea, "Can we go home?"

Once again James answered, "Tomorrow."

James doesn't remember feeling the same emotional intensity as Lisa in those early days in Moigorod. "Of the two of us, she was the missions person," he explains. "To me, it didn't matter where I served God, so it wasn't as much of a struggle. I didn't have to live overseas. I also didn't feel, *I want to go home now.*"

It took two weeks of "tomorrows" before Lisa stopped asking to go home every night. As they unpacked, the sad little apartment started to feel more like home. Getting to know people also helped pull her out of the slump.

Daily life in Moigorod still wasn't easy. The Walkers' apartment was so small they could vacuum every inch of it without changing electrical outlets. The washing machine wandered across the kitchen floor during the spin cycle and pulled its drainage hose out of the sink unless someone sat on it. Grocery stores seemed designed to prevent customers from buying things. James and Lisa had to stand in line at the counter in each department and request items by name. The salesperson would bark out a five-digit price which they were expected to remember while standing in line for the central cashier who totaled the amounts they reported on an abacus. After paying the cashier, they stood in line again at each department to show the receipt and receive their groceries—assuming they had done everything correctly. They soon learned to read an abacus upside-down to make shopping more efficient.

But the Walkers' new life also had its perks. During the gloriously long winters, a near-constant sprinkling of snow covered the industrial grime and reflected every particle of light. It was like living inside a snow globe. When the weather turned too cold for snowflakes to form and fall, the moisture froze suspended in the air, and the sky itself sparkled. Moigorod also featured a vibrant performing arts scene—a city orchestra performing classical masterpieces, one of the best ballet companies in the former Soviet Union and dance troupes representing the Slavic and Turkic minority cultures in the area. James and Lisa learned to ski, bought fur hats and drank gallons of hot, sweet tea.

After about a year in Moigorod, Lisa learned she was pregnant. Complications brought the Walkers back to the U.S. for the delivery of their son, Daniel. That's when James knew their transition to the field was complete. Lisa wanted to go home again, and this time she meant Moigorod.

THE GOOD, THE BAD AND THE SUSPICIOUS

Most of the Walkers' first two years in the field were devoted to language study and cultural adaptation. Like most cities in formerly Soviet republics in the 90s, Moigorod functioned in Russian, but it had no organized language-learning programs. James and Lisa improvised with a hodge-podge of private tutors and a few books they had brought with them or inherited from other foreigners. Just weeks after their arrival, James was asked to teach a computer course on Microsoft Windows at the training institute. He thought, "I know Windows. I can teach that," not realizing that all the labels and menus would be in Russian. Some of his first vocabulary words were the Russian equivalents of "File" and "Edit."

The Walkers' ministry efforts got off to a rocky start as well. Soon after they arrived, the government passed a law prohibiting proselytization by foreigners. It suddenly became illegal for James and Lisa to pray out loud unless a local person specifically asked them to.

They could only share their faith in response to a direct question. "It made the start of our missionary life a little bit odd," James admits. "We had thought the country was wide open for ministry, but by the time we got there, it wasn't anymore."

Despite the challenges, the Walkers were fully immersed in ministry and the local community within a few years. James summarizes life in Moigorod as "something good and something bad always happening at the same time." When the anti-proselytization law first came into effect, the Walkers were concerned. But as time went by, they saw it wasn't going to impede their ministry. If anything, the law encouraged them to work in closer partnership with the local Slavic churches so they could truthfully say, "The church asked us to do this."

The Walkers' visas were sponsored by the training institute, so James spent a lot of his time teaching English and computers. His classes provided opportunities to get to know students and share about his faith when asked. Outside of his work commitments to the institute, James helped teach local believers to share their faith, study their Bibles and plant new churches among the Turkic Muslims and other minority peoples near Moigorod. The Walkers also hosted a short-term team from the U.S. every summer and recruited teammates. By the early 2000s, the Moigorod team had grown to 10 family units. James and Lisa also added a daughter, Brittany, to their own family.

But as ministry opportunities grew, so did pressure on foreigners suspected of being missionaries. Police enforced the anti-proselytization law with enthusiasm and in some cases malice. The Walkers heard stories of authorities planting drugs on Americans and then arresting them. Rather than feeling intimidated, they became bolder. James explains, "We were trying our best to follow the law. But we decided if they wanted us gone, they would frame us for something. I would rather get kicked out of the country for doing what I came to do than for what they might make up."

It wasn't as if the police didn't know how the Walkers spent their time. Their phone was bugged. "Everybody's phone was bugged," Lisa clarifies, "It wasn't really very special." When James's dad was planning a visit, they asked him over the phone to bring a good tape measure because they hadn't found one for sale in Moigorod in three years. The following week, every store in the city suddenly stocked tape measures. Street vendors sold sunflower seeds, cigarettes and tape measures. At one point, the Walkers met a young man who said his job was to translate recordings of phone calls from English to Russian.

"Phone calls about what?" They asked in surprise. He started to recount one, then stopped abruptly and changed the subject.

"It was stressful to be under surveillance," James admits, "But you find ways to get used to it." The Walkers sometimes paused during phone calls to explain jokes or cultural references their uninvited listeners might not have understood. It didn't seem to interfere with the ministry. Lisa started an English club for moms and young children with a teatime programmed into the curriculum. She says, "We got to know the ladies and talk about their lives." For Lisa, talking about life meant talking about faith.

Through all the good and all the hard of ministry, James and Lisa felt the pressure on Christians in Moigorod, and all over the country, continue to increase. New laws were passed to limit the freedom of local believers, not just foreigners. A church was prohibited from meeting in the building they owned. They were eventually able to overturn the ban in court, but the government clearly opposed the growing Christian presence in Moigorod.

QUESTIONS AND ANSWERS

Despite—or perhaps partly because of—increasing opposition, the Walkers felt momentum building in their ministry. They had invested five years in deepening their relationships with local churches. They spoke Russian well enough to develop heart-level friendships. Their vision of reaching the Turkic Muslims in their region was just on the cusp of bearing fruit. And James and Lisa had lived in Moigorod long enough to be eligible for a five-year visa. That would save the cost and stress of frequent renewals.

Their optimism dimmed somewhat the afternoon that Anya, the office manager for the training institute, got a phone call instructing James to appear at a drab, concrete government office downtown. The appointment turned into somewhere between four and six hours of interrogation. James was provided with an official translator who seemed to relish his job when the questioning started. By the end, he just looked confused. Two uniformed officials grilled James about his activities at the institute, which he was happy to describe in detail. They also wanted to know what he did in his free time.

"You teach a pastor's class," they accused him.

"Yes, I do," James answered.

"That proves you're a missionary!"

"I am the director of the institute," James explained, "and I oversee all the programs. I use my time outside of work to teach the pastor's class."

The translator asked for clarification, "You mean it's like your hobby?"

"Sure," James told him, "You can describe it that way."

The authorities eventually let him go, but they stepped up their surveillance. Not long after the interrogation, a friend told him, "I got called in to talk about you. They told me that if I don't sign a document, they'll take away my job and my apartment." When Lisa next went for a haircut, her long-time hairdresser was called away by her boss. When she returned, the woman's chatty demeanor had vanished, and her hands trembled. In a flat, dull voice, she asked Lisa, "Who really pays you? How do you get your money?" Lisa responded that she got her money from the corner ATM like everyone else and left as soon as possible. "We felt sorry for our friends," Lisa remembers. "They felt the stress of knowing us."

A DANGER

James was summoned to the city immigration office a few weeks later. This time the Walkers both went, along with Anya and a lawyer. A woman they recognized met them in the lobby and escorted them to her office. She had befriended Lisa at a business luncheon the week before. They had made plans to get together and cook some American recipes. Now James and Lisa realized the woman was an immigration officer who had been surveilling them. She looked uncomfortable as she informed James that he was being deported as a "Danger to the Republic."

James asked what laws he had broken. She said the relevant laws were classified and instructed him to sign a document acknowledging the charge. For a moment, James considered not cooperating. "What if I don't?" he asked.

The officer looked even more unhappy. "In a few days, the police will come to your house and put you in prison."

"Honey, that is not an option," Lisa told him firmly.

Anya agreed. "You'll disappear, and we'll never hear from you again."

With the lawyer's help, James wrote on the document, in Russian, that he didn't agree with the statement and was signing it under duress. He added his signature on top of that text so it would be difficult to alter.

The immigration official told James he had 10 days to leave the country, but she emphasized to Lisa, "You're not being deported, so you don't have to leave."

"Do you think I'd stay here without my husband?" Lisa asked in shock. "I'm just sorry we won't get to cook together after all."

James and Lisa rode home from the immigration office in a daze. When they shared the news with their friends and family in the U.S., one of the responses they heard was, "It's fine. You can come home now. You did your thing." Lisa bristled at that. She had just lost her house. Her friends. Her job. She didn't think she could handle returning to the U.S., where people would tell her, "It's good that you're home. Now you're safe." So, standing in their little Soviet kitchen next to the roaming washing machine, Lisa asked James, "What if we don't go back to America?"

They decided to ask their area leader, based in Western Europe, if they could come to his city temporarily to figure out what to do next instead of returning to the U.S. He agreed with their plan immediately over the phone. Western Europe would be their "strategic waiting place" long before anyone used that term.

A GUARDED GOODBYE

Lisa describes their last 10 days in Moigorod as "unbearable." They had to hurriedly hand over the leadership of their ministries to teammates and local believers. Over the next few years, all 10 foreign families on their team would gradually be pushed out of Moigorod, all for different reasons and often with little warning.

The Walkers packed two suitcases per person to take with them to Europe—mainly clothes, photos and keepsakes. They also stored some boxes for a friend to ship to them once they'd resettled. Brittany was only one, too little to feel much attachment to anything except her family. But Daniel was three, and he sobbed as he watched his toys disappear into boxes. James and Lisa made sure to pack his favorite Thomas the Tank Engine train and one circle of track in their luggage, but the rest had to go into storage.

Partway through the Walkers' 10-day departure period, a uniformed guard appeared at the entrance to their apartment block with the tip of a machine gun sticking out of his black duffel bag. Lisa called a teammate and told her, "The kids and I are coming to stay at your house. My babies can't handle all this pressure of watching us give away their things." James finished emptying the apartment and met the rest of the family at the train station.

Even then, the wonderful and menacing aspects of life in Moigorod continued to coexist side-by-side. All the Walkers' local friends gathered on the train platform to say goodbye. While they wept, sang hymns and pressed notes into James and Lisa's hands, the armed guard hovered in the background. A teammate accompanied the Walkers to the capital to help manage the kids and luggage, but the train supervisor had clearly been warned about them. Every time they opened the door of their cabin, she rushed up to ask, "What are you doing?" and block the exit.

When they finally reached the airport, the Walkers stuffed as many heavy things as they could into their stroller and the pockets of their winter coats to keep their suitcases under the weight limit. Then they walked through passport control one last time. James and Lisa wouldn't get to be "lifers" in Moigorod after all, but they hoped to find a new chapter of missionary service somewhere else, maybe with less orange-and-purple wallpaper.

Of War & Wallpaper

James & Lisa Walker's Story
Part 2

GRIEF UPON GRIEF

The Walkers landed in Western Europe in a heap of luggage and emotions. A ministry leader picked them up at the airport and hosted them in his home for their first week. Other missionaries pitched in to help as well. One family invited Lisa over to do laundry every week. Others helped them rent a tiny, two-room apartment and loaned them furniture and dishes. James and Lisa anticipated a transition period of about six months, which was all they could afford. The financial support they had raised met their needs in the former Soviet Union, but Western Europe was significantly more expensive.

Little Daniel had been droopy through the whole transition, so when they moved into their apartment, Lisa decided to cook one of his Moigorod favorites—a stuffed pasta dish—to cheer him up. As she puts it, "You don't like to see depressed three-year-olds." That reminder of home brought out all the accumulated emotions of the past several weeks. Daniel sat on the living room floor pushing his one Thomas train around and around the little circle of track, sobbing.

James and Lisa tried to comfort him, but they were struggling too. Even before the deportation, Lisa had already been grieving the loss of her mother, who died earlier that year. And then, just weeks after arriving in Europe, the Walkers saw Moigorod in the news and learned that one of the women from Lisa's English club was killed, along with her children, in a house fire. Grief piled on top of grief.

James doesn't remember questioning whether their time in Moigorod had been wasted, but Lisa often wondered, *What were those five years of my life for?* She didn't think of it as a bad experience. Despite the inconveniences and surveillance, she missed Moigorod. But she wondered, *What was God's purpose?* When people checked in on Lisa, she told them, "I don't know how I'm doing, but I know that God is good."

One friend pushed back a little, "Is that what you really feel, or are you just saying it?"

So, she was honest. "I'm just saying it! My feelings are too much, so all I can do is repeat the truth I know."

James says faith was a choice during that season of uncertainty. "We decided, *God is good. We'll make it through this.*"

FACTS AND FICTIONS

A big part of "making it through this" was figuring out what would come next. The Walkers hoped to resettle in a European or former Soviet context rather than start over in a completely new culture. Since Daniel had developed asthma like his dad, they needed to be in a place with relatively clean air and a good level of medical care.

Just a few days after they arrived from Moigorod, the Walkers' area leader pulled out a map of Europe and explained where other teams were based, what sort of ministries they engaged in and where he would like to see new teams form. About six weeks later, James and Lisa started taking survey trips to potential locations. None of them seemed like a good fit. The Walkers narrowed their list to two options that felt possible, but still not quite right—one in the Balkans and one in Central Europe. Neither country was Russian-speaking, and neither had a Pioneers team.

Logically, the Balkan country had more needs. There were fewer missionaries, fewer believers and significant problems within the existing church leadership. The work there felt both compelling and daunting. The second option, in Central Europe, had all the emotional appeal. James had family heritage there and Lisa had always been drawn to it. They connected well with missionaries from other organizations. But during their visit, the air pollution triggered asthma attacks for both James and Daniel and the Walkers thought, *We can't live in a place where we can't breathe.*

James resigned himself to serving in the statistically needier country with better air. While he wrote a newsletter at the Pioneers Europe office to announce their decision to go to the Balkans, Lisa called her sister Janet, who lived in Europe, to explain their thought process. Lisa admitted they were making the decision based on the numbers. Janet responded that their Central European option also had a massive spiritual need, even if the statistics were not as bleak as those for the Balkans. She also pointed out that they had visited an industrial region of Central Europe. That explained the poor air quality. There were plenty of other cities where James and Daniel would be able to breathe freely.

With those significant but somewhat surface arguments against Central Europe set aside, Lisa finally grappled with the underlying reason they were hesitant to go there: It felt too nice. Life in Central Europe didn't seem hard enough to be a real ministry, and it would be significantly more expensive than Moigorod. Janet responded bluntly,

"That's a really dumb reason not to go somewhere. If the Lord is calling you there, He'll help you raise the financial support you need."

So, Lisa called James at the office and told him, "You can go to the Balkans, but I'm going to Central Europe." She meant it light-heart-edly—sort of—but the truth was, both James and Lisa *wanted* to move to Central Europe. "You can't really say you love a place when you've only visited it once," Lisa admits, "But we felt the beginning of that in our hearts. We hadn't felt that way about the other country. We were just looking at facts and figures." They talked through it again, and Lisa persuaded James. He deleted the word "Balkans" from the newsletter, replaced it with "Central Europe," and clicked "Send."

MISSIONS 2.0

The Walkers would be the first Pioneers missionaries in their new context, but they didn't feel alone. Experienced workers from other organizations offered direction and support. And for James, starting something new was attractive. They had essentially started a new team in Moigorod and had enjoyed it.

The finances of permanently relocating to Europe still felt like a huge obstacle, but the Lord provided just as Janet had assured them He would. The Walkers' sending church contributed an extra $10,000, which allowed them to furnish their new home. Friends joined their financial support team and others increased their giving. "I can't say it was easy," James reflects, "but the Lord provided what we needed to make the move."

Lisa remembers an overall feeling of hopefulness. "I think the Lord helped me be ready for the challenge. He put in my heart a sense of adventure once again. A lot of people, if they thought they were going to have to learn another language, would feel discouraged. But for me, it was more like, *Wow, I can learn this one better, maybe more systematically. I guess we get a 2.0.* And I felt less scared than when we went to Moigorod." *We've done it once, we can do it again,* the Walkers reasoned, and not in a self-sufficient sense. They just felt the Lord was going to help them through the transition. They were right.

DREAMS AND DOUBTS

Lisa describes language learning in Central Europe as a dream. "We just signed up, and there we were in a class!" James wasn't quite as excited about starting over in a new language, but he was grateful that the university had a formal program and that the language shared Slavic roots and some general grammatical framework with Russian. For extra language practice, the Walkers hired a private tutor. She found it hilarious to hear Americans speak her language with a Russian accent.

When James and Lisa were practicing expressing likes and dislikes, their tutor asked, "What do you *not* like about living here?" They responded with blank looks. "No really," she urged, "Tell me. I can take it." But James and Lisa couldn't come up with a single negative thing to say. They tried to explain, in their limited vocabulary, that they had come from living in a tiny Soviet apartment under constant surveillance to a beautiful home in a free society, and they honestly loved everything about it.

The Central European lifestyle they had feared would be "too nice" turned out to be a blessing. They had rented a spacious house with a fenced-in yard. Their city had grocery stores where you pushed a cart down the aisle and filled it with the things you wanted. No more reading an abacus upside-down! Daniel happily attended a preschool run by a Christian family, where he made friends and started picking up the language. James found the relative modernity of their new town calming. "We could even go to McDonald's if we wanted to."

When Lisa looks back on that first year in Central Europe, she describes it as "this cushion of feeling delighted that had an underside to it. I almost felt survivor's guilt. Like maybe I wasn't as much of a missionary anymore." It didn't help that some friends from Moigorod visited them and immediately concluded, "Oh I see—now you're going to have a ministry among rich people."

The Walkers also began to feel a disconnect with the other missionaries in the area. "Our experiences were so different from theirs, it almost felt like we didn't speak the same language. We would worry about getting kicked out and they would look at us like, *What? That doesn't happen.*" But it *had* happened to the Walkers, and the effects lingered. In some ways, they still lived like they were under surveillance, always anticipating a knock at the door and a police officer outside to question them.

James explains, "It's not paranoia if people are actually out to get you. We were coming out of a situation in Moigorod where people became our friends simply to report on us. When we moved to Central Europe, we were still carrying that mentality with us and had to recalibrate." James and Lisa didn't notice the effect until a local pastor commented, "We hope that someday you are able to relax and trust us." They didn't mean to be distant or suspicious, but their cautious attitude showed.

The Walkers felt somewhat safer after their neighbor shared that when they first moved into their house, the police had called her with questions about them. "I don't have to answer any of this," she had told them, "Go away!" And that was the end of it. A civilian could never have responded to the authorities like that in Moigorod. Slowly, it began to sink in for James and Lisa. *We're okay. No one is going to come and kick us out.*

OKAY TO NOT BE OKAY

In early 2003, after a year in Central Europe, the Walkers decided to make a trip back to the U.S. to visit their families and the prayer and financial supporters who undergirded their ministry. It was already hard to leave their new home. James and Lisa were getting to know people. Their local church invited them to work with the youth group, which they loved. The kids were doing well. But they felt it was time to go back and thank everyone for so generously supporting them through the transition.

The Walkers borrowed a Ford Fiesta and drove through 17 states with two toddlers, staying a night or two at a time on friends' couches along the way, eating fast food and drinking too much caffeine. "It was an insane trip," James admits. Eventually, they made their way to Florida for some vacation time with Lisa's family.

Just as they started to settle in and relax, Lisa woke up in the middle of the night thinking she was having a heart attack. James raced her to the ER, but it turned out to be a false alarm. Lisa managed to get a little sleep in the early morning hours, but she woke up to a seemingly endless series of anxiety attacks. "They were like waves, and they wouldn't stop. I would get maybe a five-minute interval before the next one just crashed over me." Everything in the room grew distant like an out-of-body experience and blood pounded in her ears. She couldn't even read her Bible for comfort. "I could look at words, but my brain wasn't capable of deciphering them."

Lisa had never suffered from anxiety before. She called a counselor who specialized in missionary care and was able to meet with him that afternoon. The first thing she said was, "Please don't make me stay in Florida. That would be the worst thing for me. I'll do anything. Just let me go home." By home, she meant Central Europe.

The onset of the anxiety attacks at the end of a really good year seemed bizarre to Lisa at first. The counselor helped her understand that the accumulated trauma of the previous two years—the death of her mom, the grief of their abrupt departure from Moigorod, news of house fire deaths right afterward, the prolonged uncertainty of the transition, and the stress of a new language and culture—had all finally built up and overwhelmed her. Lisa explains, "I had pushed all the sadness aside because I needed to get where we were going next. I couldn't begin to think about it, so I didn't. Now I had to. I tend to power through stress, but my body decided for me that I couldn't do it anymore."

To Lisa's enormous relief, the counselor was willing to help her build a care plan she could implement in Central Europe, where she felt settled and at home. Her recovery included medication, rest, exercise, diet changes and regular check-ins with the counselor and a medical doctor. At home in Central Europe, Lisa could fix healthy meals in her own kitchen and put the kids down for naps in their own beds. After about nine months, she started to feel like herself again. Looking back at that period, Lisa reflects, "I came to understand that even though the ending was okay, we had still experienced a trauma. The Lord was good to us, and He provided. But it was still okay to say, *I'm exhausted.*"

READY AND WILLING

The Walkers continued to deepen their roots and their ministry in Central Europe for the next two decades. They worked alongside local churches, discipling believers and sharing their faith. They encouraged the vastly outnumbered Christians to reach out to their neighbors and helped them study God's Word. James and Lisa found the work rewarding and fulfilling, but also challenging. At one point, their local church went through a particularly difficult season and the Walkers felt overwhelmed as they tried to help members heal from hurt, anger and a sense of betrayal. "It was ugly," James remembers. The Walkers shared the challenging situation with a visiting missionary.

"You know what you need?" he told them. "You need to go to a place where you can be successful."

James and Lisa sat around the kitchen table long after he left and considered his advice. In the end, they decided, "That's not what we want. We don't want to be successful. We want to be where God wants us."

Once they were well-established in their town and ministry, James and Lisa were asked to take on a leadership role within Pioneers. They would oversee missionary teams in six European countries. It was a very different role than James, in particular, had pictured for himself. His understanding of what God wants from him has changed since he first went to the mission field in 1995. "In my mind back then, I was a teacher, a youth worker, a discipler kind of person. I was willing to go anywhere to do those things. Much of our ministry in Moigorod and here in Central Europe matched that. I can't say where along the line the transition began, but God showed me I'm called to serve Him wherever He sends me and do whatever He asks me to do, regardless of whether or not it fits who I think I am."

And for the foreseeable future, God seems to want the Walkers to stay in Central Europe. Every two years, they used to renew their residency permit. In 2014, as they began the familiar process, an immigration officer suggested that if they wanted to stay long-term, they should apply for citizenship. Instead of the typical long, expensive immigration process, he recommended that they apply directly to the country's president. "Write him about why you want to be citizens," he told James and Lisa. "He can accept or deny you. It won't cost anything except the stamps."

So, the Walkers gathered documentation of why they wanted to be dual citizens of the U.S. and their adopted country. James included a seven-generation family ancestry chart tracing his heritage to Central Europe. Friends, neighbors and the kids' teachers wrote letters in support of their application. The town mayor provided a formal reference embossed with a gold stamp. "They were rooting for us," Lisa explains. "They had seen our children grow up. In some ways that town is our hometown, as much as anywhere has ever felt like a hometown to me."

A few months later, Lisa burst into tears of joy and relief when a government official informed her over the phone that all four of them had been granted citizenship by the president himself. The Walkers might have a reason to leave Central Europe someday, but they can't get kicked out, ever. Daniel and Brittany eventually moved back to the U.S. for college, but they still consider a small town in Central Europe their hometown.

"We aren't the best missionaries ever," James admits. "We are probably near the bottom level, not the higher end. We're doing the best we can with what God has given us to do. The one thing that has kept us here until now and will always keep us is a sense of, *God, You called us here, so we will do what You give us to do.*"

Early in the morning on February 24th, 2022, God gave the Walkers something new to do for Him.

Of War & Wallpaper

James & Lisa Walker's Story
Part 3

ON WAR'S DOORSTEP

In the late 90s and early 2000s, the Church in Ukraine flourished in both faith and numbers. When Russia invaded in February of 2022, thousands and then millions of Ukrainian civilians fled west across the border into Central Europe. Christian organizations and churches in Ukraine stepped up to care for their communities during the crisis and organize evacuation routes. Ministries in Europe mobilized to receive the refugees. And in the Walkers' adopted country, some church leaders estimated there were twice as many Ukrainian Christians as local believers by April.

For the last two decades, James and Lisa had intentionally kept a low profile in the Christian community in Central Europe. They partnered closely with local churches but didn't attend denominational gatherings or hold leadership positions, except within Pioneers. They adopted that approach because of their experience in Moigorod, where church politics often led to possessiveness toward missionaries and their resources. When the war started, James realized that keeping his distance from denominational leadership meant he now had little credibility at a time when networking and relationship became essential. "Without really knowing it, we applied what we learned culturally in one situation to our new situation, not realizing it was a misapplication. I wish I could do that all over again."

But the Walkers were still well-known in the missionary community. Friends of friends called at all hours asking them to pick up refugees crossing the border, which was just over an hour away. Vans organized by Ukrainian churches dropped groups off at their door to wait for transportation farther west. James describes it as "an ad hoc, informal network from five different organizations. You called who you knew. If I couldn't help, I directed them to someone else." The Walkers decided to only host people in their home who were referred by a friend or a Christian organization. They helped others with supplies, meals and transportation as they were able.

SOUP AND TEARS

For weeks, James and Lisa woke every morning to phone calls and young children either playing or crying. In three months, they hosted more than 150 people and their pets. Most stayed only a few nights before moving on to friends, relatives or resettlement centers. "The first wave of people stood in line at the border for days," Lisa says. "When they arrived, they were cold. The children were freaked out. Some hadn't eaten properly. Some arrived sick. A few older people seemed to have dementia and looked terrified." A 14-year-old boy declared he wouldn't eat until he was taken home. His family went on to Spain, and Lisa hopes he didn't maintain his hunger strike for too long. "Grief manifests in different ways. He had no aspirations of going back to fight. He just wanted to go back and die like everyone else. Not exactly the thoughts you would expect to hear from a junior high boy."

The majority of the refugees spoke Russian, even if it wasn't their first language, so the Walkers strained to dredge up a language they hadn't spoken much in 20 years. James says, "When I was with Ukrainians, I could usually at least catch what they were saying. With Google's help, I could communicate back. I would look at the word on my phone and remember, *Oh, that's right!* and then I could say it."

Lisa's sister Janet came for a few weeks to help manage the flow of people. They developed a system for welcoming up to 15 refugees at a time. On quiet days, Lisa cooked and froze huge batches of dill pickle soup, a Central European comfort food. When a group arrived, Janet heated the soup, cut bread and distributed bowls. James handed out towels and managed the shower rotation. Lisa, whose Russian language came back faster, sat at the kitchen table listening to the refugees share their stories, which she found difficult both linguistically and emotionally.

"They often showed me pictures of bloody bodies. I was able to understand enough Russian to have empathy and hug them and tell them it was terrible. And I communicated with them about where they needed to go next. I remember thinking, *I could not be getting through this right now if the Lord were not helping bring language back to my mind. I don't really know these words, but here they are, coming out of my mouth.* People were patient with me because they could tell I was trying."

The strain was significant, especially because Lisa is an introvert. "I'm not that person who's like, 'Everybody come on in! Let me make soup!' It was more like, *O Lord, help me make the soup and help me get through talking to all these people and listening to their heartbreaking stories.* That's what God did with our lives and our home."

A STORY WITHOUT AN ENDING

While the Walkers willingly opened their home to strangers, they also had the joy of reuniting with a close friend from Moigorod. A local believer named Masha had worked with James at the institute and kept in touch with Lisa ever since. For the last few years, she had left her homeland to join a ministry in Ukraine. In the early days of the war, she was too afraid to flee. Eventually, though, she called the Walkers to say she was on a bus headed toward the border.

"We cried at the news," Lisa remembers. "We told her, 'We will be here to greet you!'"

The Walkers had no idea how long it would take Masha's bus to reach the border. James drove to the crossing at 9:30 that night to wait by the side of the main road. As the night wore on, he struggled to stay awake. If he missed the bus, it would take Masha to the next city, six hours away, where there would be no one to meet her. James started a cycle of setting an alarm, sleeping for an hour, and then waking up to check his phone for any communication from Masha. He didn't hear from her until 11 a.m. Just after noon, she finally stepped down off the bus on the side of the road where James had been waiting for 15 hours. "Both she and I cried because God had answered our prayers and brought her out."

A few days later, Lisa drove Masha to the capital so she could fly to Israel, where her son now pastored a messianic church. "I think I had a deeper conversation in Russian with Masha on that two-hour drive than the whole time I lived in Moigorod. The Lord just opened up my mind and her mind, too, I'm sure, to fill in the gaps of what I was trying to say." Lisa remembers thinking at the time, *The Lord is doing this. I have this Russian somewhere in this head of mine, and He's bringing it up so I can be here for Masha.*

Masha also felt a deeper connection with Lisa. "I guess I'm kind of feeling what you felt when you were deported," Masha said. "I mean, we were sad when it happened, but we never really thought about all you went through." She was right that the Walkers' experience of being displaced connected them with the Ukrainians they served. James clarifies, "It's not that we've 'been there done that,' but we tried to go as far down the extra mile as we could because we understood what it meant to be forced to leave your home. I remember arriving in Europe from Moigorod and thinking, *What are we going to do now? Where are we going to live?* At least we had an income and knew someone who took us in."

James is also cautious about exaggerating their role in the Ukrainian refugee crisis. "In the context of all the other stories of what was going on, ours is tiny. I don't feel like we did anything anybody else wouldn't do."

By the end of May 2022, the number of Ukrainian refugees crossing the border each day dwindled and the Walkers decided they no longer needed to keep their home set up as a transit center. They took down most of the beds at their house and packed away the extra linens. Most government and non-profit reception centers had closed. Aid workers and equipment moved on to address other crises. The Walkers were impressed with the generosity of their community, but realized, "People have reached the extent of what they feel they can give and do."

But the refugee crisis wasn't over. A year after the start of the war, the Walkers were still trying to find help for 15 Ukrainians living in a rundown house on the edge of town because the refugee center shut down. "This isn't a story with a bow at the end of it," Lisa says. "There's a Ukrainian girl with leukemia living in a really bad house and her mom has no job. And it's not like there's going to be more help coming. When we say we're done, we're probably some people's last stand."

STEWARDING THE UNKNOWN

In all the twists and turns of their missionary lives over the last 25-plus years, the Walkers have noticed a theme: "When things really get hard and difficult, you have a choice to shut down or to see where God is leading." In each hard experience, they have seen God's goodness. That doesn't cancel out the pain or the loss, but it does strengthen their faith.

James says, "I've become less long-range in my planning, and more faithful to what God has given me to do rather than faithful to what I hope I will be doing. When we went to Moigorod, we thought, *We'll be here for a long time.* We had great plans, but God didn't want us there for a long time. It all just—boom!—fell apart. Then we came here to Central Europe, and it's been a long time. We focus much less on what happens five years from now and more on, *Am I doing what God wants me to do today, in this moment?* It's not like I've mastered it. But I now realize where I'm failing faster."

From Lisa's perspective, "We're trained to be strategic, but our strategies sometimes completely fall apart. I've learned to be more accepting of that. Instead of thinking, *What are my goals?* I now ask, *What has God given me stewardship over?* That's helped me, a planner who has been disappointed on many fronts, to cope when goals don't come to fruition."

The Walkers are learning to live in contentment with what the Lord has given them now and to trust Him with the big picture of His purpose—even when that purpose includes deportation, war and terrible wallpaper.

Epilogue

A Pickle Soup Prayer Group

THE STORIES IN THIS BOOK are just a tiny sampling of the experiences of missionaries on the move. These five have been drawn from all over the globe and cover a timespan of about 30 years. One of the common themes in all the stories is how the community of believers provided guidance, encouragement and comfort in times of transition. Throughout history, God's people have met to pray and fellowship and eat. We invite you to continue that tradition by gathering a group of believing friends over a meal to share what you've read.

Below is Lisa Walker's recipe for the dill pickle soup she served by the gallon to Ukrainian refugees in the first months of the war. While pickles and soup may sound like an odd combination to American ears, this is a beloved comfort food across much of Central Europe. Even if pickles aren't your favorite, we encourage you to give the tangy, creamy hug-in-a-bowl a try. There are as many variations of this soup as there are Central European cooks, so feel free to experiment while using this basic version as a starting point.

Most importantly, don't eat pickle soup alone! This recipe serves eight, so invite some adventuresome friends to join you and share the stories that inspired the menu. When you've sopped up the last of the broth, spend some time in prayer together. Here are some ideas of things to pray for to get you started:

- Hope, safety and gospel access for the millions of people who have been driven from their homes due to war, famine and persecution.

- Comfort, courage and wisdom for missionaries who have been displaced from their countries of service.

- Creativity and perseverance for displaced missionaries resettling in new locations overseas or back in their home countries. Many are learning new languages and adapting to new cultures and ministry contexts.

- Wisdom for parents helping children through transitions and new friends for the whole family.

- For the global Church to demonstrate a flexible and responsive faith as the world changes rapidly around us.

- For God to show you, and your local church, how you might more effectively serve missionaries and refugees in light of recent world events. What opportunities might He be revealing? What challenges will you have to overcome?

Lisa Walker's Dill Pickle Soup

Serves 8. We recommend adding some warm, crusty bread and butter on the side.

INGREDIENTS

4 tbsp butter

2 medium onions

2 cups grated carrots (about 2 large carrots)

2 cups grated or chopped dill pickles (see the note below)

6 medium potatoes

10 cups vegetable or chicken broth

½ cup sour cream

4 tbsp flour

6-8 tbsp pickle juice (from the pickle jar)

1½ tsp salt

½ tsp black pepper

8 tbsp fresh dill

OPTIONAL ADD-INS

Parsnip, garlic or celery (add with the carrots)

Bay leaves (add with the broth)

Cooked chicken or ground beef (add near the end)

A note about the pickles: Choose dill pickles that are more briny than vinegary. Polish dill pickles and kosher dill pickles usually work well, even if they include some vinegar. They can be grated or chopped.

STOVETOP INSTRUCTIONS (1 HOUR)

1. Chop 2 medium onions.
2. Grate or finely chop the carrots and pickles (about 2 cups of each).
3. In the bottom of a large soup pot (6-7 quarts), sauté the onion, carrots and pickles in 4 tbsp of butter for about five minutes.
4. Meanwhile, cube 6 medium potatoes (peel them if you prefer).
5. When the sautéing veggies are slightly soft, add 10 cups of broth to the pot and bring it to a boil.
6. Add the potatoes and simmer for 10 minutes.
7. While the soup cooks, whisk together ½ cup of sour cream, 4 tbsp of flour and 6 tbsp (½ cup) of pickle juice in a small bowl. Stir in a few spoonfuls of hot broth so the sour cream won't curdle when you add it to the soup.
8. Add 1½ tsp of salt, tsp of pepper and the sour cream mixture to the soup and simmer another five minutes, or until the potatoes are tender.
9. Taste the broth and add more pickle juice 1 tbsp at a time if desired (a little bit goes a long way).
10. Serve immediately, garnished with fresh dill.

SLOW COOKER INSTRUCTIONS (4.5 HOURS)

1. Chop 2 medium onions.
2. Grate or finely chop the carrots and pickles (about 2 cups of each).

3. Cube 6 medium potatoes (peel them if you prefer).

4. Add all the ingredients except the sour cream, flour and fresh dill to your slow cooker (4 tbsp butter, 2 onions, 2 cups carrots, 2 cups pickles, 6 potatoes, 10 cups broth, 6 tbsp pickle juice, 2 tsp salt, ½ tsp pepper).

5. Cook on high for four hours (until the vegetables are tender).

6. Whisk together ½ cup of sour cream and 4 tbsp of flour in a small bowl. Stir in a few spoonfuls of hot broth so the sour cream won't curdle when you add it to the soup.

7. Add the sour cream mixture into the slow cooker and simmer for a few more minutes.

8. Taste the broth and add more pickle juice 1 tbsp at a time if desired (a little bit goes a long way).

9. Serve garnished with fresh dill.

Scan the QR code or go to Pioneers.org/PickleSoup to print a copy of this recipe.

About Maxine McDonald

Like most of the names in this book, Maxine McDonald is a pseudonym. Maxine has had the privilege of participating in global missions in five countries. She has served with Pioneers since 2013 and now writes and edits books for adults and children. Maxine enjoys telling the stories of how God is using His people to build His Church among all the many peoples of the world.